INSIDE
FOREIGN AID

Also by Judith Tendler
Electric Power in Brazil: Entrepreneurship in the Public Sector

Judith Tendler

INSIDE
FOREIGN AID

The Johns Hopkins University Press
BALTIMORE & LONDON

Manufactured in the United States of America.

The Johns Hopkins University Press, Baltimore, Maryland 21218
The Johns Hopkins Press Ltd., London

Originally published, 1975

Johns Hopkins paperback edition, 1977

Library of Congress Catalog Card Number 75-11353
ISBN 0-8018-1731-5
ISBN 0-8018-2016-2 (paperback)

Library of Congress Cataloging in Publication data
will be found on the last printed page of this book.

TO MOLLIE MEDOW TENDLER,

my mother

Contents

CONTENTS

Acknowledgments

Much of this study is based on observations made during three years of work as an economist with the U.S. Agency for International Development (AID). Two of the three years were spent at the Brazil Mission in Rio de Janeiro (1967-68) and one year in Washington with the Latin America Bureau (1969), including field work in Ecuador and Costa Rica. The Center for Latin American Studies of the University of California at Berkeley generously supported part of my research and writing, and the Center for Advanced Study in the Behavioral Sciences at Stanford provided me a gracious setting for the rest. Neither the Centers nor the Agency is responsible for my opinions or information.

For secretarial help, I am beholden to Dorothy Brothers of the Center for Advanced Studies and to Ann de Peyster. Thanks also to Ann and Roxanne Bartlett for proofreading and to JoAnn Gutin for editorial help. For dedicated critical attention to the manuscript, I am most grateful to Max Hall, Bruce Johnston, Martin Krieger, Arthur Stinchcombe, Aaron Wildavsky, and an anonymous reader. They will find that I failed to allay several doubts.

For living very much with me and not with my book, I owe the most to Richard Chambers. My children, Rebecca, Stephen, and Karen Chambers, grew strong and beautiful while I was working.

Judith Tendler
Berkeley, California
February 1975

Abbreviations

ABDIB	Associação Brasileira da Defesa de Indústrias de Base
AID	Agency for International Development
CANAMBRA	Canada-America-Brazil (a consortium of private consulting firms set up to prepare a plan for expansion of electric power facilities in south-central Brazil)
GAO	Government Accounting Office
GEIMEC	Grupo Executivo da Indústria de Máquinas e Equipamento de Construção (Executive Group for the Heavy Construction Equipment Industry)
IBRD	International Bank for Reconstruction and Development
IDB	Inter-American Development Bank
UNDP	United Nations Development Program

INSIDE
FOREIGN AID

Chapter One

INTRODUCTION

Criticism of aid started in the 60s

This volume was inspired by the spate of official evaluations of development assistance programs commissioned in the late nineteen-sixties.[1] The reports echoed, in milder form, much of the criticism directed at development assistance for some time by aid receivers and others.[2] I agreed with most of the criticisms, which are summarized below. Yet the remedies proposed by official and nonofficial commentators reflected a perception of the world of development assistance that was, to my mind, incomplete. Certain problems seemed to go unnoticed. Some organizational features were judged undesirable which, in my view, seemed desirable. Many of the proposed changes seemed certain not to produce the desired results. What seemed missing, in brief, was a sense of the organizational setting in which assistance decisions took place. I wanted to extend the discussion of development assistance by looking at the organization from inside its own walls, to show how the organizational environment had contributed to the outcomes described in the official and unofficial reports.

Most of the criticism of development assistance can be summed up in five categories: (1) assistance too often takes the form of unnecessarily large capital projects, overly intensive in equipment and foreign exchange; (2) the technology of such projects has often been too sophisticated to be absorbed by developing-country institutions; (3) the design and execution of financed projects has too often coin-

1

cided with the interests of developed-country firms in the business of exporting consulting services and equipment; (4) in the case of U.S. bilateral aid, legislative and administrative requirements have been imposed which make the program look more like an attempt to subsidize U.S. exports than an effort to assist less-developed countries to grow; (5) the "ugly American"[3] type of professional is a final contributor to the problem, because of his tendency to think that his country's way of doing things is best. These problems have long been more vigorously described by some aided countries as donor-country hypocrisy, export dumping, "gravy trains" for donor-country consulting and exporting forms, imperialism, or neocolonialism.

Based on these diagnoses, it is usually prescribed (1) that a larger share of development assistance be channeled through multilateral institutions in order to cleanse it of the political and business interferences of a bilateral program; (2) that liberalization of donor-country trade policy be considered essential to any aid program promoting growth in the less-developed world; (3) that donor-country institutions make diligent attempts to learn how to simplify technology; (4) that procedures for evaluating a proposed project be streamlined and improved in order to select projects and project designs better suited to the priorities and resources of the aided country; (5) that better technicians be hired, and that aid-giving institutions train them in the special techniques of development assistance; and lastly (6) that developed-country technicians attempt to be less "ugly."

What distinguishes my study from the above discussions is my portrayal of the organizational environment as playing a central role in determining the content of development assistance programs. I see organizational factors as responsible for outcomes that are usually considered the result of other things — policy directives, political pressures, employee training, project analysis techniques. Other discussions, for example, explain how better analytical techniques improve the quality of project selection. This study, in contrast, focuses on the overriding influence exerted on project selection by the way in which organizational output gets defined. Whereas other studies focus on the constraining effect of policies imposed by the legislative and executive branches, this study looks at the way in which the organization adapts to such constraints and how this adaptation gets incorporated into organizational behavior. Whereas other studies stress the problem of insensitive technicians and the need to recruit *focus on*

and train better ones, this study explores how the ~~organizational environment~~ itself attracts the insensitive technician. Whereas other studies question the political motives behind development assistance, this study explores the possibility that genuine motives get crossed up by the needs of the organization to gain control over its environment. This study, in short, analyzes assistance programs in terms of the deterministic nature of their task, task environment, and organizational design.[4] It attempts to find the organizational rationality that lurks behind much of the behavior of development assistance organizations.

The difficulty of tracing today's development assistance problems back to these organizational factors explains to a certain extent why critics have singled out other, more visible causes: bureaucratic inefficiency, pressure by developed-country manufacturers with equipment to sell, political payoffs, underdeveloped-country irrationality, technical incompetence, or masked neocolonialist motives. Most such explanations, unlike those relating to the organizational setting, point to highly visible groups who have been known to behave on other occasions in the criticized way. These explanations fit in with theories, accepted in one quarter or another, about how certain types of groups or countries behave. I do not deny the value of these explanations, but suggest that they have been hit upon first because they are more visible and correspond to existing analytical approaches to organizational and political behavior.

Some of the problems outlined above belong solely to the U.S. bilateral program and its executor, the Agency for International Development (AID). The attempt to explain AID's problems often centers on the subjection of that agency to the pressures of private interest groups and to poaching by other government entities. Most public sector entities, however, are subject to some form of external buffeting, so that this explanation does not tell us enough about this particular organization. One wants to know more about how the organization dealt with such assaults — in short, how it coped with the normal pressures of the bureaucratic scene.[5]

Equally fragmentary is the finding that AID's bureaucracy was insensitive, overlarge, and unadaptive. That is how bureaucracies often turn out to be.[6] Indeed, when adaptive and innovative behavior does occur in an organization, it is often analyzed in terms of the organizational characteristics that enable the entity to overcome the lethargy and resistance to change that is inherent in any bureaucracy.[7] One wants to know, then, how and why the innovators and risk-takers in AID were kept from playing their role. Did the agency's environment spurn them? If not, there is even more reason to be curious about why the forces of lethargy and resistance prevailed.

AID started out with some characteristics unusual for a public sector bureaucracy. This endowment, unnoted by evaluators, seemed particularly suited to a task like development assistance — a task that was far outside the range of the typical functions performed by most public sector bureaucracies. In fact, the U.S. organization may have started out better fit for the task at hand than the less-maligned multilateral agencies — the International Bank for Reconstruction and Development (IBRD), the United Nations Development Program (UNDP), and regional banks such as the Inter-American Development Bank (IDB). The disappointing performance of the U.S. agency, in sum, was particularly interesting, given the fact that it had started with a better than even organizational chance for success.

In observing AID from within, one is taken with the intricacies of a bilateral foreign aid organization subject to the slings and arrows of the rest of the government to which it belongs. Only after a time does it become apparent that many of the more important "bilaterally-caused" problems of U.S. foreign aid are prevalent in the *multilateral* organizations as well. This is surprising not only because the problems seem such an obvious result of bilateralism but because "multilateralization" has been proposed for some time as one of the most potent methods for improving the quality of U.S. foreign assistance. It is supposed to rescue the donor organization from the undermining influences of U.S. political and national security goals, U.S. business pressure on the design of projects and decisions, and congressional hostility to foreign aid. Yet, if a certain type of problem behavior is found in any assistance organization, regardless of its remoteness from national entanglements, then the vaunted multilateralization does not necessarily make inroads on some of the criticized problems.

The intent of this inquiry, then, is twofold: to explore the unique character of the Agency for International Development as a public sector organization, and to analyze certain problems which, although most visible in the highly bilateral context of one particular agency, turn out to afflict other types of development assistance organizations as well. The first three chapters concentrate on the bilateral AID. The next three extend the discussion to phenomena pervading both bilateral and multilateral organizations. The IBRD, or World Bank, has become the most significant lender of development assistance funds in the nineteen-seventies, and the IDB is the largest and oldest of the regional development banks. Though of lesser significance, the UNDP is brought into the discussion partly because of the excellent description of its organizational environment in the Jackson Report, revealing that it was characterized by some of the same organizational problems that occurred in IBRD, IDB, and AID. Though the UNDP differs from these other organizations because it specializes in technical assistance and feasibility studies, it plays an important role as supplier of financeable projects to these organizations and, despite its differentness, has experienced remarkably similar organizational problems.

The IDB is a unique hybrid of multilateralism, bilateralism, and regionalism. Unlike the IBRD, it is staffed in large part by recipient-country technicians, which introduces politics into decisionmaking in a way that is distinct from both AID and IBRD. Unlike AID, moreover, the IDB's contributors are multinational, although all are within the Western hemisphere. Since its largest contributor is the United States, moreover, the organization is subject to AID-like bilateral forces; but these forces are much less intense and determining than those involving AID.

The differences between IDB, IBRD, and UNDP — and the way these differences relate to their funding arrangements — are discussed at length in the literature.[8] I treat all three organizations as "multilateral" — even though their differences may describe them better than their shared multilateralism — because I am interested in certain behaviors usually considered bilateral. At the same time, I point out their differences to show that certain organizational traits occur across a quite varied array of institutions dealing with development assistance.

A good part of the thinking in this book grew out of my association with the Latin America program of AID, particularly in Brazil, in the late nineteen-sixties. Much of the illustrative material reflects that association. The book, however, is not about AID's Latin America program. It is an attempt to say something general about development assistance organizations, based on a learning that could only have taken place through close involvement with one part of a large organization. During and after my AID-Latin America years, I had considerable exposure to AID programs in other regions, and to other assistance organizations, which provided an opportunity to check my perceptions. Where possible, I have incorporated supporting material from the literature of these other programs and places, though I have not attempted to prove my analysis with systematic data from other countries and other organizations. I have enlisted my experience to concretize and enrich the argument and to lead the reader up to propositions that might otherwise seem preposterous.

Since my original experience with AID, its appropriations and personnel have been on the wane, while the IBRD has moved in the opposite direction. Between 1967 and 1974, the IBRD's loan commitments quadrupled, rising from $1.1 billion to $4.3 billion. During the same period, the funds appropriated for U.S. foreign aid declined by 20 percent, from $2.1 billion to $1.7 billion. Correspondingly, AID cut its personnel by half, from 17,600 direct-hire Americans and foreign nationals in 1968 to 9,400 in 1974. At the same time, the IBRD more than doubled its professional staff, from 734 to 1,752.[9] As a result of these transitions, the discussion of AID in the following three chapters may be more relevant to the IBRD than would have been the case some years ago. At the same time that AID starts to retreat from its decentralized system of resident field missions, for example, the once-centralized IBRD begins to look with more favor on the idea of establishing such missions. Other changes have been taking place in development assistance organizations — whether they are waxing or waning — such as the new concern with employment generation and income distribution. I have discussed these processes of change in the text wherever they enhance or modify my original argument.

Finally, most of the decisionmaking discussed in the book refers to project lending — though program lending receives explicit attention on pages 96 and 97. The IDB does not make program loans, and most IBRD activity is concentrated in project lending, with less than 5 percent of its 1974 commitments in program loans.[10] Though program lending has accounted for as much as 50 percent of AID's development lending, its share has decreased since 1969 to less than 10 percent of the proposed budget for fiscal year 1975. Sector loans have also become important in AID, accounting for 50 percent of the program in 1974 and 90 percent in 1975.[11] Although this approach represents a significant attempt to plan at sector rather than project levels, the sector loan is, to a certain extent, no more than a new way of grouping individual projects for presentation purposes. In that sector loans consist of a package of discrete projects, then, what is said here about project lending applies to sector lending as well. Similarly, technical assistance activities are relevant to my discussion in that they are often directed toward generating applications for project financing. I concentrate on project lending, therefore, because it accounts for the major part of resources committed and a more than proportionate number of personnel. As a result, the project loan has had much more influence than the program loan in structuring the environment of development assistance organizations.

Chapter Two

THE TASK AND THE ORGANIZATIONAL FIT

The U.S. foreign aid agency was a quite special case of public sector bureaucracy. It had a decentralized structure and small familylike field missions, in combination with a remarkably present-oriented personnel system. All this contributed to an organizational environment that permitted considerable mobility, informality of communication and decisionmaking, and easy access to the top. This type of environment, in turn, was suited to organizational tasks which, like development assistance, tend to require a more than average amount of adaptive and innovative behavior. Certain features of AID's structure and personnel policies, then, seemed to have endowed it with a high probability of success. This unusual combination of organizational characteristics, along with an equally unusual task, has not attracted the attention of the analysts of organizations and bureaucratic behavior.

Although the agency's organizational environment was more conducive than most to adaptation and innovation, criticism of its performance has often focused on its unadaptive and uninnovative behavior. The reason the agency's performance fell short of its seeming fitness for the task is the subject of the next three chapters. This chapter describes the special nature of the demands made by the development assistance task on a public sector institution and the almost inadvertent aptness for that task of AID's organizational design.

THE NATURE OF THE TASK

One of the most distinguishing characteristics of the work of a foreign aid agency is its differentness from that of other government bureaucracies operating abroad or other money-spending bureaucracies at home. Like other public works entities, for example, AID has to spend money on highways and housing. But the typical highway or low-income housing project it finances will turn out wrong if done "by the book." The highway will fall apart long before the end of its service life because of lack of maintenance and vehicle load control practices in the aid-recipient country. Poor people may move into the housing project only at gunpoint, because that way of living seems so alien. Yet the foreign aid agency is held accountable if the highway falls apart or if the housing project remains unoccupied. At the same time, the agency may be just as censured for using procedures that strayed, in the interest of innovation, from standard technical norms.

Although the uniqueness of the foreign aid agency's task has been recognized and understood,[1] the organizational environment that such a task requires has never been specified. Nor has it been understood how the organization's inability to provide such an environment can contribute just as much to its ineffectiveness as can the pressures of outside interest groups, the insensitivity of the ethnocentric technician, and the restrictiveness of the legislature. When a task is different from most, and relatively new, there will be little technique to deal with it. The literature on the subject will be limited, the accumulated experience within government will be sparse, and the capacity of other government entities to carry out their normal watchdog functions will be meagerly developed. The routine response as a form of bureaucratic action will not work as well as in most large organizations. Familiar problem-solving techniques and activities will often be insufficient to carry out the task. The problem may require not only untried techniques of solution, but may first have to be sought out and defined — a kind of searching that is alien to much professional training in the developed world.[2] The task of development assistance, then, involves not only "doing." An essential portion of it has to do with learning.[3]

Because of the peculiar nature of the development assistance task, the written word will have special importance within the organization. Written chronicles of the agency's experience and analysis of what has been done will be needed much more than in a home-based bureaucracy, where sure prescriptions for well-defined problems abound and where a general literature on how things work is usually available. Hence the agency's own writing will be an important medium through which a body of knowledge will be built up concerning the task at hand — knowledge that will help the organization to be less dependent on the erratic appearance of individual innovation.

The special character of the foreign aid agency's task requires that the organization have the proper atmosphere for groping without too much idea of what will result, for straying from tried and true solutions, and for struggling to escape from customary ways of thinking about things. The agency will need a number of bureaucrats with a penchant for this type of behavior; and an organizational environment will have to exist to which such types are attracted, in which they can make cohesive and informal groups, and in which they are able to gain power.

Although all this may seem obvious, its practical implications are directly contrary to the argument used to justify the responsibility of developed countries to aid the less-developed world. For I have been saying that the atmosphere of a development assistance agency has much in common with that of a less-developed country starting out on the path of development: wide gaps in experience and knowledge of the problems confronted and a corresponding maze of bureaucratic procedures that seem to provide an essential protection to the bureaucrat from the uncertainty and opaqueness of the world about him. Making things even more difficult for the assistance technician or administrator than for his recipient-country counterpart is the fact that the former lacks the native person's feel for what will work and what will not. Regardless of such difficulties, however, development assistance was established on the premise that the developed world possessed both the talent and the capital for helping backward countries to develop. Development know-how was spoken about as if it were like capital — a stock of goods capable of being transferred from its owners to the less privileged.[4] But development knowledge is not simply a stock with transferable properties. The peculiar nature of the development task makes knowledge a *product* of the transfer experience itself.

This augmented definition of development assistance — where the transferred resource is both input *and* output of the transfer process — makes it difficult to provide as clear a rationale for the assistance as underlies the commitment to transfer capital. For knowledge that is still to be learned cannot, by definition, be more abundant in one part of the world than in another.[5] The difficulty of reconciling the rationale for development assistance with the need of the assistance organization for learning space can perhaps be attributed to the fact that our culture "does not contain concepts for simultaneously thinking about rationality and indeterminateness."[6] In practical terms, this difficulty has constituted a significant impediment to allowing these organizations to grope as much as they needed to. In order to maintain credibility with Congress, public watchdog entities, and investors (in the case of the multilateral banks), the organization could not admit that it often had to thrash around for solutions. Conversely, the pat technical solution was often slapped on a problem that might require another, less charted approach — sometimes in an inadvertent retreat from the uncertainty of less tried and true techniques.[7]

A result of the difficulty of accepting and putting into practice the augmented definition of development assistance is that when problems arise, they are attributed to the wrong causes — causes that fit the knowledge-as-stock definition of assistance. If an attempt to transfer a stock of knowledge to the underdeveloped world does not work well, the problem is said to result from imperfections in the transfer mechanism — inadequately trained technicians, counterproductive bureaucratic procedures, the impingement of forces from without — rather than from an organizational environment that does not generate its share of the skill to be transferred.

As a result of this narrow definition of knowledge transfer, the recommendations that accompany the evaluations of development assistance seem to be founded on an unlimited faith in the ability of developed-country man to cope with less-developed-country problems — a faith that is very much a result of the analysis of the failure. That is, put developed-country man in a streamlined organization, remove counterproductive outside pressures and legislative constraints, train him to be less ethnocentric, improve the techniques he must use, give him intense training in these techniques — and he and his organization will be much better fit to carry out the task at hand. If, however, a good part of the task is learning and adapting, then a good part of the burden rests on the organization and not the individual: he will not be better at development, no matter what his training, unless the organization is set up in a way that requires learning as an output.

The rationale behind development assistance, in sum, causes donor organizations to surround themselves with a protective aura of technical competence — an aura which must be maintained if they are to survive in their institutional world. This makes it difficult to generate the experimental environment necessary for their work. It also tends to result in placing the blame for failure on the wrong thing.

THE ORGANIZATIONAL FIT

The literature of organizations has shown that a certain type of organizational structure has been most conducive to the accomplishment of a task like development assistance, where "problems and requirements for action arise which cannot be broken down and distributed among specialist roles within a clearly defined hierarchy."[8] The organizational structure indicated is decentralized, with superior-subordinate demarcations blurred, access to superiors easy, and considerable responsibility assumed by subordinates. The environment of AID fits this organizational description well. The agency's geographical dispersion and small field missions required a decentralized structure with considerable delegation of responsibility. Certain personnel policies had the same effect, although they were designed, as will be seen, with other purposes in mind.

The blurring of hierarchical lines in AID was partly a result of gaping vacuums of knowledge and power at various points in the organization. To a considerable extent, the agency was peopled with organizational types who were self-effacing, back-stepping, and apologetic. One did not often hear an AID professional express pride at working for the agency or speak contemptuously of other federal bureaucracies. (Perhaps the latter is a better measure of an organization's self-confidence.) Professionals at the IBRD, in contrast, would regularly exhibit amused scorn for the technical competence of their AID or IDB counterparts. Budget Bureau technicians, too, displayed an elitist self-confidence in their organization and a disdain for the abilities of the government entities they were overseeing. In AID, it was common for some of the brightest and most successful professionals and administrators to let it be thought that they were looking for positions elsewhere, even when they were making no serious efforts to leave. They thus managed to withhold their respect from the agency while continuing to work for it. A good part of the characteristic AID humility expressed itself in relation to Congress, particularly at low levels of the organization and early stages of project design. At such points, a new idea was more frequently scrapped with "what would Congress say?" — than adopted with the attitude of "how could we get this one around Congress?"

The new recruit to the agency was often surprised to sit down at his first meetings and discover people who were not intrigued with the process of economic development, who were ground down and exhausted by their bouts with developing-country environments, and who were not curious about the inner workings of their organization's successes and failures. They seemed to find a certain degree of comfort and enjoyment in each other's company, engaging in a kind of friendly griping about the "beneficiary" and his world. The innovator, in turn, was accepted almost with relief by his peers and superiors, since he could often produce what they could not. His job description, salary grade, or administrative rank did not matter. His intrusions into the territory of others would often be requested; or he would, on his own, step into the vacuum left by tired or frightened colleagues.[9] What was unique to AID was not a more than proportionate share of the latter bureaucratic type but rather an extremely challenging and frustrating task environment. The faces of AID probably looked about the same as those of any large, home-based federal bureaucracy. It was the world they had to work with that made them timid.

The agency's decentralized structure and dispersion abroad in independent, familylike country missions also contributed to the unusual fluidity of vertical and horizontal movement within the organization. It was not simply a matter of the smallness of the organizational subunits. Their location in a foreign country — often looked upon by the staff as an alien environment — meant that the work unit doubled as a kind of social unit. This contributed to a more casual atmosphere at work, which, in turn, facilitated accessibility.[10] The informality was not necessarily a sole function of decentralization into small independent units. Similar dispersion abroad, in the embassies of the State Department, produced just the opposite result: an even more hierarchical environment than in the headquarters organization in Washington.[11] It was the combination of decentralization with other factors, discussed below, that seems to have produced the less hierarchical result in the case of AID.

The system of decentralized country missions increased the opportunities for a staff member's mobility not only because of the small, familylike nature of the individual unit. Equally important was the possibility of moving from one mission to the other. The agency's encouragement of such rotation through its designation of two-year "tours of duty" made it possible for the staff member who could not get what he wanted in his own mission to try his fortunes in another — thereby increasing his expectation of possible promotion or reassignment as a reward for his efforts. The constant rotation between missions meant that positions were always being vacated and chances were always occurring to move up. Hence the high rate of inter-mission and field-Washington mobility removed one disadvantage of the small unit — the difficulty of moving upward, or even sideward, because of the smallness of the organization.

The high incidence of rotation in AID and the State Department has usually been noted because of its unfavorable side: moving people from one place to another just as they are getting to know a country — or, perhaps more accurate for AID, *allowing* them to move. As seen above, however, the rotations that occurred in the agency were not all that arbitrary and disadvantageous.[12] The employee himself had considerable interest in moving about, and the most successful ones were usually entreated by the country mission to renew their tours rather than rotate. An important aspect of rotation, then, was that it counterbalanced the tendency of a large public sector bureaucracy to offer little hope for rapid recognition and promotion.

Also contributing to the possibilities for action and power by the interested AID innovator was the uniquely present-oriented cast of the agency's personnel system. The legislative authority for AID's foreign service personnel system (Sec. 625[d] of the Foreign Assistance Act of 1961 as amended) — as well as that of its predecessor agencies — was based on the Foreign Service Act of 1946 as amended. AID was enabled by the legislation to employ most of its professional American personnel for overseas service under a rubric little used until recently by the State Department's Foreign Service — namely, the Foreign Service Reserve (FSR). This category had been designed to give the State Department and pre-AID entities the authority to hire professionals "on a temporary basis . . . with such specialized skills as may from time to time be required" (Sec. 401[3] of FSA of 1946). The time limit imposed on such employment was two non-consecutive five-year periods (Sec. 522). In AID's case, however, the time period was "the duration of operations" of the agency (Sec. 625[d] of FAA of 1961). In effect, this allowed the agency to employ people indefinitely without giving them the normal employment security accorded Civil Service employees (e.g., seniority rights and veteran's preference during times of personnel reorganizations or reductions), Foreign Service Officers, or even the FSR officers of the State Department.[13] Moreover, unlike the Foreign Service Officer, the FSR officer was not required to take rigorous entrance exams.

The orientation of the foreign aid bureaucracy was exactly opposite to that of the career Foreign Service of the State Department. Because the same type of criticism has often been leveled at the two groups, as if they were one, it is useful to clarify this significant difference in their organizational environment. Unlike AID, the State Department's Foreign Service is imbued with the atmosphere of an elite career service.[14] As one would expect in such a service, criticism and inno-vational behavior suffer because of the young officer's long-run in-terest in advancing his career.[15] Entry is limited by a tough written and oral exam. A period of initial work well below the level of the young officer's interests, aspirations, and talents is the usual rule. The initial apprenticeship period is tolerable to the recruit presumably because his career promises a future of power, prestige, and adventure — and because his acceptance into this elite corps confers immediate prestige on him in the eyes of the outside world.[16]

AID and its predecessors, in contrast, have always been much less future-oriented employers, even in comparison to federal bureauc-racies without a career orientation like that of the Foreign Service. AID was created in 1962 in order to, among other things, put together under one roof some of the previously dispersed foreign assistance activities of the government — the International Cooperation Ad-ministration, the Development Loan Fund, the Food for Peace Pro-gram, and the local currency-lending activities of the Export-Import Bank. The agency's attitudes about personnel corresponded to the manner in which it had committed itself to development assistance — as if it were a task like the Marshall Plan, something that could be terminated with success in a five- or ten-year period. "I don't think it will happen for 10, 15, 20 years perhaps," said the agency's adminis-trator in 1963, in response to a question about whether the program would terminate after some specified period. "But it certainly will terminate in many places before then, and it may terminate com-pletely before then. The personnel system that is used must be com-patible with the possibility of terminating any part or all of the program which may not last too long."[17] Of course, the placing of a terminal date on the assistance commitment may have been more a political maneuver on the part of aid proponents than a realistic assessment of what would happen. Aid proponents were said to have calculated that Congress would never authorize the funds unless it was promised that the program would eventually come to an end, sooner rather than later.[18] Whatever the case may have been, it was always clear to the agency that its existence would come into question by Congress as soon as the end of that temporary period came near.

The agency, then, could not honestly promise a long-term career to its job applicants. Unlike the State Department, it was not interested in entrance exams. Whereas the separateness of the State Department's Foreign Service personnel system was meant to serve the purpose of creating an elite career corps, the reasons for a separate foreign aid personnel system were just the *opposite*: to be able to get already trained and experienced people fast and at the same time be free of the Civil-Service-type employment obligations to them.[19]

In 1963, more than half of the agency's overseas staff (1800 out of 3300 Foreign Service Reserve positions) had limited-tenure appointments, meaning that they would gain tenure after an initial trial period of arbitrary length only with the agency's specific approval.[20] Moreover, almost half of the agency's American personnel abroad in 1968 were not direct-hire; they were either on loan from other government agencies or on contract — and hence were employed for limited periods of time. Finally, the agency did not request authority to include its personnel in a career system until 1966 because, according to its own rationale, it was engaged in a temporary task.[21] All this seems rather unusual behavior for a public sector bureaucracy which has been criticized for having been ossified and unadaptive.

The career horizon of the foreign aid employer and employee, then, was atypically short. People were expected to perform immediately and be rewarded immediately. In contrast to the Foreign Service, there was no time for, or value placed upon, rising up from the bottom and getting one's experience that way. The employee expected his job to bestow on him immediately the responsibility and discretion that his experience merited. People tended to find their levels on their own — without as much resorting to formal reassignments, promotion, reorganizations, or job redefinitions as in other federal bureaucracies. Those who could not cope gravitated toward more secure "paper-pushing" functions, and those who were interested "took over" very soon after entering. The unusually short-term career horizon of the agency and its employees meant that the fear of stepping out of line, and of what it would do to one's career, did not pervade the organization the way it did the Foreign Service. At the least, such fear was not a constraining element for those who were interested in experimenting or changing existing practices.

The relative absence of hierarchy and excessive preoccupation with promotion in AID must have had a positive effect on the agency's ability to carry out its task. Its overseas technicians, that is, could perform best if they got out into the culture of the country where they worked and got to know its people. If they were preoccupied with rising up in the ranks, however, they would consider it important to spend more time with those who would help their ascendancy moves —i.e., other Americans. The type of activity that led to promotion in the more rank-oriented Foreign Service of the State Department, as one observer has pointed out, had little to do with the ability to speak foreign languages and develop social relations with host country nationals, or with the knowledge of foreign cultures and political patterns. Specifically, "the important social contacts for the American diplomat who wishes to rise in the hierarchy are those with other Americans, both important American visitors and members of the American missions. Too much association with natives is likely to involve some slighting of this relationship to other Americans, and is, consequently, likely to retard promotion."[22] AID's fluid environment and ease of promotion, in contrast, must have been an important liberating factor, in the sense that overseas employees would not be sacrificing so much in terms of career opportunity by spending time with the people of their host country.

AID appeared to be unique, then, in setting the scene for a dedicated, risk-courting corps of technicians clever enough to pursue the goals of their organization and at the same time defend it from attempted incursions from the outside. The organization was fitted out with some atypical characteristics, which seemed, almost fortuitously, just what was needed for the atypical task at hand. This potential for healthiness in the AID environment stands out even more clearly when contrasted with the analyses of lack-of-innovation problems in the future-oriented ranks of the State Department.[23]

The State Department, interestingly, resorted more and more to the reserve category originally used mainly by AID and predecessors, rather than the more elitist career-oriented Foreign Service Officer category. In 1959, FSR accounted for 28 percent of the total number of new FSO and FSR appointments, and 38 percent in 1961; [24] in 1968, FSR's were 36 percent of the total number of FSO and FSR staff members. The Herter Report stated that the FSR category had become "the primary vehicle for obtaining needed skills at intermediate and higher professional levels in the State Deparment."[25] Indeed, recent evaluations of the State Department's Foreign Service recommended that some of its "creativity" problems be remedied by modifying the recruitment system in a way that made it look more like AID's tempo- rary foreign service. The State Department Task Force on the Stimula- tion of Creativity recommended that the department allow officers "to be released for up to 4 years to pursue brief careers elsewhere in government and in other professions . . . with provision to return to the Service without prejudice to their careers."[26] An article in the journal of the Foreign Service Officer's Association recommended the end of the FSO career service and its replacement with the recruit- ment of experienced professionals.[27] In sum, the State Department's elite Foreign Service, in attempting to deal with its own lack of innovation and adaptiveness, was advocating personnel changes which would make the service more like the non-elitist AID.[28]

Although I have characterized the agency's present-oriented per- sonnel system as desirable, most of the attention focused on this system was of a critical nature. As early as 1962, for example, a report on foreign affairs personnel concluded that "the failure to establish a recognized career service and professional status for persons engaged in foreign assistance work" was the main cause of difficulty in recruit- ing high quality personnel.[29] In 1965, the Foreign Service Journal editorialized: "If there is one agency in the foreign affairs field in which greater administrative flexibility, unity and order in personnel matters are required, it is certainly AID. Many officers are on limited FSR appointment. No permanent appointments to AID's career ser- vice have been made since 1961. There is a hodge-podge of personnel systems with FSO, FSR, FSR (limited), AD (Administratively Deter- mined), and Civil Service ratings, derived from a variety of legislative sources."[30] In 1968, a report commissioned by the American Foreign Service Association said that the major contribution of "the able and dedicated staff of AID and its predecessor agencies" to American foreign policy was "all the more significant" because this personnel "has been denied coverage under a stable personnel system."[31] In 1969 the agency was complaining to the Congress that its lack of a career system and its temporary status were obstacles to recruitment.[32] The agency's rate of turnover was said to be higher than that of other government agencies — 25 percent as compared to 20 percent — and this allegedly reflected the general level of employment insecurity.[33]

The Agency's temporary status was criticized for its effect not only on staff recruitment and morale but also on the organization's ability to carry out its unique task. "It is perhaps inescapable," said the report of a congressional committee evaluating AID personnel administration and operations, "that the hasty manner in which it was necessary for this country to organize and staff the successive foreign assistance programs and to continue changing programs and key personnel to meet changing conditions, would eventually create a large, amorphous, unstable agency, which would provide one of the most serious handicaps in carrying out the complex foreign assistance programs."[34] Likewise, an ex-member of the Nine Wise Men, President Kennedy's *ad hoc* advisory committee on Latin American policy, recounted that the Alliance for Progress operated "as if it were likely to go out of business at any moment. . . . As a result . . . it functions like a disorganized ministry in a poor and backward country."[35] The author goes on to say that this problem resulted in a lack of the use of modern management and policy tools and a "shoving into the background" of the problems of information and research.

The short-term career horizon, then, may not have had as positive an effect as I have described. It may actually have caused the kind of job insecurity that prevents the development of adaptive, innovative behavior — and it may explain to a certain extent why the agency was not blessed with more of such behavior. Security is necessary to ensure the potential experimenter that he can take unpopular stands, sometimes fail, and go out on a limb without losing his job. Just as important, such security facilitates the formation of informal groups within the organization, for employees feel less need to compete with their colleagues "when promotions and dismissals depend on explicit and openly announced standards."[36]

Piecemeal organizational approaches and frequent changes, however, do not necessarily bring on the type of inadequate performance that AID critics have described. After all, stable and long-lived government bureaucracies with secure personnel systems have been criticized for the same lack of adaptive behavior and experience, but the shortcomings have been attributed in these cases to *excessive* security and stability. The rigidity of the Foreign Service, in the works cited above, is seen as a consequence of the fact that it is an age-old entrenched organization, insulated from the forces of change by the timelessness of its values and career system.

An example of the potentially positive results of organizational newness and insecurity is the Latin American experience with autonomous state companies — the so-called mixed companies. The evolution of this particular organizational form in the public sector has in many cases constituted a significant breakthrough for government action in developing countries. The mixed company successes, however, were based on the same organizational characteristics which were considered to have caused the problems of AID. That is, the successful mixed companies frequently started out without much structure or security, made up of the better personnel of the government ministries from which they had broken away. Their ability to free themselves of particularly cumbersome civil service and procurement procedures was of major importance, especially in that this allowed rapid hiring and the paying of attractive salaries. The success of these new organizations, then, was their very newness, their manning by persons who had previously worked in the same branch of the public sector, and their breaking away from the more constraining aspects of government bureaucracy.

Although the analogy between the mixed company and AID is not completely fitting, it at least shows that we cannot accept "organizational disorder" and "temporariness" as "obvious" explanations for the problems of AID. Indeed, one of the reports that criticized the impermanent nature of AID's personnel system suggested elsewhere that career stability was probably not a desirable feature for the personnel system of an organization carrying out a task like development assistance:

The requirements of AID's program preclude a permanent career service because the needs for specialized personnel abroad change every year. . . . Better personnel will be obtained by hiring persons for temporary tours of duty. They will be forced to identify with their profession. . . . The decisive reason not to include these specialists in an AID career system is that, in the main, the career contexts and career loyalties of the best professionals lie with their professions and the whole range of activities with which those professions are associated. An association with AID, even if it could be made permanent, would not attract very many of the best professionals to spend most of their working lives overseas, far from their professional colleagues and the stimulus of professional association.[37]

In addition, it seems that the insecurity of the AID personnel system as it existed on paper had not been reflected in the amount of firing and "removal of deadwood" that one would expect. The Herter Report suggested that the temporary "reserve" designation of AID foreign service officers was really "a misnomer in terms of its originally intended use as a temporary hiring device" because Foreign Service Reserve appointments in AID could be made for the duration of the agency's operations. In the State Department, in contrast, such appointments were limited to a given period of time. Hence, "a substantial portion of AID's Reserve officers have been with the Agency and its predecessors for many years. . . . Clearly, the Agency has a substantial nucleus of what amount to career personnel even in the absence of a formally constituted career service."[38]

Any government job offers what might be called informal security — as opposed to the formal security of being a member of a particular federal bureaucracy. The civil servant who distinguishes himself in a government job automatically becomes highly eligible in the eyes of other government entities. He is noticed and may receive job offers from these entities, especially if his work involves contact with them. Thus, if his agency is on the wane, this type of person is usually in an excellent position to find a good place in another government bureau. Some agencies are looked upon by ambitious young professionals as a way to establish their reputations for future opportunities in the political, business, or government world. AID in particular was considered this way, especially by lawyers, partly because of the high possibilities for mobility described above.[39]

Finally, the AID environment was an insecure one only in relation to other Civil Service departments. With respect to the private sector, the AID employee was still considerably more secure. There was a significant difference, moreover, between the reaction of the ambitious or competent bureaucrat and that of the less competent one to threatened personnel reductions. The latter lived through such periods with great fear, much talk of what would happen, and resentment at the insecurity of the work environment. The former, in contrast, would sometimes even welcome the rumors of personnel reduction because of the opportunity "to get rid of deadwood," or they would pay the rumors little heed, secure in the knowledge that they would not be touched. Or, when the program was threatened with complete demise, they would joke about the fact that the only result would be "a changing of acronyms" for the agency — and that they expected to take the same place in the newly-initialed entity, whatever form it might take.[40]

In conclusion, one has to look beyond the obvious explanation of chaos and insecurity in order to find the reasons for AID's problems. Chaos and insecurity may have been an integral part of an organizational environment that was better equipped than most for coping with the job of development assistance.

Chapter Three

THE MISFIT

*takes an org.
approach.
org theory?
bureaucracy*

Certain development assistance problems are commonly explained in terms of the ethnocentricity of the developed-world technician, his insensitivity to other cultures, and his inability to meet the challenge of new situations. This chapter, in contrast, shows that AID's structure and task environment made it almost inevitable that certain problems usually attributed to individuals or a culture would have surfaced in any case as organizational phenomena. The task at hand required an organizational environment that could produce learning; the organizational level at which learning behavior was required was much lower, or at different points, than in a more typical government bureaucracy; and the type of person recruited for these positions was no different from those recruited for similar-level and similar-function positions in a home-based bureaucracy, where routine behavior at these levels is more functional.

BOTTOMHEAVINESS

AID differed from home-based government bureaucracies in that a major input into the program had to come from those outside it: either the recipient governments or other local borrower groups. This crucial beneficiary input into the production of development assistance was made at the organization's far-flung outposts — the country missions — rather than in conjunction with headquarters personnel in Washington. Recipient-country technicians, in short, usually worked side by side with AID counterparts who were far removed, geographically and hierarchically, from positions of power. This geographical distance almost fortuitously bestowed discretion on the AID field technician. He had considerable latitude in making decisions about project design and in accepting or rejecting suggestions from the recipient about such design. It was not only decentralization and dependency on recipient-country input that caused this greater discretion; equally important, the state of knowledge in the field of development precluded the possibility of defining problems and tasks in a standardized way at the organization's apex.

Because most of the daily interaction between borrower government and lending agency occurred geographically distant from Washington headquarters — and with the outposts of the organization rather than with its center — the "bottom levels" were very important in the designing of loan programs. The organization, therefore, was forced to be particularly reliant on its lower ranks for adaptive and innovative behavior. Yet these were the levels least likely to produce such behavior. The job position was usually technical and nonadministrative, occupied by a person who was accustomed, by rank or by profession, to dealing with routine problems by way of routine responses.[1]

Another factor contributing to AID "bottomheaviness" was the nature of the interagency struggle in Washington. Many of the constraints on AID action were imposed by other federal entities charged with overseeing certain aspects of the foreign aid program. The degree to which these constraints were exercised was very much dependent on changing power constellations, on changing degrees of support from the executive, and on changing economic conditions (such as balance-of-payments improvements). The institutionalization of these constraints in the hands of other federal offices endowed these bodies with a degree of informal control over AID. The way they exercised this control was often unpredictable; it could change with a change in personnel, and its extent was frequently revealed to the agency in particular cases only after a complex process of negotiation and bargaining. (See chapter 4 for further discussion of these points.)

Because of the nature of these outside constraints and their determination by events in Washington, it was difficult for the technician living in the field to have an up-to-date idea of what he could "get away with." If the mission had been accustomed to getting a lashing from Congress or the Treasury on a particular issue in the past, then

the technician would tend to avoid that approach automatically —
even if it was most economic from the aided country's point of view,
and even though, unbeknownst to him, it may have been clear to
AID-Washington officialdom that the constraining entity was currently in a more lenient mood. Although the Washington staff attempted to maintain a continuous flow of current information to the missions, it was difficult to prevent a kind of safe-for-all-occasions,
problem-avoiding behavior at the outpost level. Moreover, the preoccupation of the Washington staff with its interagency struggles cut
deeply into the time it had to work on substantive policy problems.
Hence Washington was not completely free to become interested and
involved in policy issues arising from the field, even if such issues
were regularly brought to its attention. Robert Wood describes a
somewhat similar phenomenon occurring between the executive office staff and the executive agencies:

Operational matters flow to the top — as central staffs become engrossed in
subduing outlying bureaucracies — and policy-making emerges at the bottom. At the top minor problems squeeze out major ones, and individuals
lower down the echelons who have the time for reflection and mischief-
making take up issues of fundamental philosophical and political significance.[2]

The result of AID bottomheaviness, then, was that the higher-level
Washington administrator could not always be aware of the risk-
avoiding behavior that might underlie many of the technical decisions embodied in the design of a project. Even though he might have
been willing to fight for an issue with an outside agency — or even
though he might have known that prevailing moods had changed — it
was difficult for him to be aware of past rejections of optimum choices
at technical levels far removed from him in space and rank.

In sum, AID's task differed significantly from that of a home-based
moneyspending bureaucracy in two ways, both of which tended to
place an excessive burden on the organization's lower levels for
innovative and adaptive behavior. First, the beneficiary of the program was far away and, at the same time, was a crucial and unpredictable contributor to the organization's output. Second, the nature of
the organization's work was less understood than that of a home-
based bureaucracy, so goals were not easily translatable into
problem-solving tasks. Thus while the decentralized structure of AID
and its intimate country missions contributed to the ease of mobility
and operation within the organization, decentralization also tended
to inhibit the very type of behavior needed for the task at hand.

HEADQUARTERS AND FIELD

One more aspect of AID's decentralization tended to impede the growth of an adaptive organizational environment: the friction between headquarters and field, which often stifled the exchange of information and help. In the average AID country mission, "Washington" was griped about as the source of a merciless flow of requests for reporting, an unreasonable setter of time deadlines, a faraway bureaucracy with no comprehension of the problems of working with developing-country institutions with no sense of deadline. Missions often talked of Washington not as their harassed ally, manning the front lines of defense against the rest of government, but as one of their harassers.

Washington, in turn, often talked of a mission as if it were a stumbling, wayward lamb, which could not follow the simplest instructions and got itself into unbelievable messes. "I don't know what they've been doing down there all this time!" was an oft-heard comment of exasperation in Washington. In a similar vein, the AID Administrator commented in a congressional hearing that mission personnel "get what is commonly referred to in our agency as 'localitis', and they may very well be pushing programs, projects, and policies which a cooler judgment, a broader vision, indicate are not all that important."[3]

Much of the Washington-mission irritation can be classed as the internal family squabbling and banter characteristic of most decentralized organizations.[4] Nevertheless, each party's distrust of the other's competence and comprehension tended to produce a self-protective and devious quality in the mission's dealings with Washington and a correspondingly impatient and unanalytical attitude in Washington toward problems encountered in the field. As a result, there were many mission-level problems that Washington did not hear about. Though some of these unaired problems concerned relatively minor issues, they were nevertheless important because of their role in the "from-the-ground-up" evolution of practices and policies. In sum, the part of the organization which had greater familiarity with the constraints of other entities, greater power to deal with them, and a valuable overhead of multi-country experience, was not brought to bear as much as it should have been on the important activities carried out by its less knowing, more fearful branches.

COHESIVENESS ABROAD

In attempting to describe the agency's problems in carrying out its task, one cannot neglect the effects of placing a self-contained professional and social group in a foreign country. The cliquishness of Americans abroad — or, for that matter, any diplomatic group in a foreign country — is well known. Less documented is the effect that such immigrant groupings seem to have on the professional life of the bureaucrat living abroad. Technicians working out of AID field missions were often surrounded by an aura of professional outdatedness, isolation, and bureaucratic timidity.[5] This professional atmosphere seemed to be part of a general "immigrant" style of life, rather than the simple result of professionals being separated from libraries, colleagues, and organizations which, like Washington headquarters, had more of an overview of development experience. The professional outdatedness seemed to go along with the slightly passé clothing of the AID employees and their wives, the lack of involvement in what was happening in their host country or home country, and a kind of folksiness associated with an earlier, smalltown America.

These American AID groups abroad remind one of the "fragments" described by Louis Hartz in his analysis of the evolution of countries colonized from Europe. "When part of a . . . nation is detached from the whole of it and hurled outward onto new soil," he writes, "it loses the stimulus toward change that the whole provides. It lapses into a kind of immobility." Although the fragments reflect every phase of the social and political changes occurring in the mother country, "they evince alike the immobilities of fragmentation. . . . There is a stifling of the future as well as an escape from the past, and it is at the heart of the process of fragmentation that one is determined by the other."[6] Like these same fragments, the American foreign aid groups located abroad seemed to exhibit traces of their mother-country civilization without having any of its motive energy. An ex-AID administrator makes remarkably similar observations about the U.S. Foreign Service abroad, in commenting on the aloofness of Foreign Service Officers toward AID people and programs. "Few foreign service officers were truly comfortable with the proselytizing thrust of the Alliance [for Progress]. Having spent years abroad, relatively out of touch with the burning issues of political reform, civil rights and poverty at home, professionally trained to hold aloof from domestic politics, they were alienated from the reform spirit of their own culture."[7]

My analogy with the Hartz description stops at the point where the very process of being extricated from the mother country gives the fragment, as he says, the freedom to evolve. "By extricating the European ideologies from the European battle, by cutting short the process of renewal which keeps that battle going, they [the fragments] permit precisely that unfolding of potentialities which the Old World denies."[8] The Americans abroad, however, did not seem to develop or even possess the Hartzian potential resulting from their detachment.

The distinct nature of the AID "fragment" abroad can be better understood by referring to our knowledge of immigrant groups. The two groups, of course, are basically different: AID employees came to the new country with a secure job and knew they would one day return home, while immigrant groups have usually faced great employment insecurity, knowing they had no alternative but to make a way in the new country. The relevance of the comparison, however, lies in the fact that cliquishness in the two groups has been judged in totally different ways. The stigmatization of immigrants by the society around them, and the consequent sticking together of alien groups, has been considered a source of *strength* in the literature on immigrants. This outcast status has been pointed to as a partial explanation of the contribution that such groups have made to the development of a country.[9] The American foreign aid "immigrants," in contrast, are *taken to task* for sticking together, and their clannishness is felt to impede their contribution to the host country.

The reason for this striking difference in the two valuations of cliquishness is perhaps to be found in the type of contribution attributed to each group. The immigrant groups are studied, and their cohesiveness emphasized, when they have made a contribution that arose from their differentness — e.g., the successful introduction of a new type of product, such as the cultivation of fruits and vegetables in Brazil by the Japanese. Cliquishness, in other words, made it possible to cope with an alien environment and maintain differentness — and, in turn, to institutionalize some aspect of that differentness into a new productive activity.

The foreign aid group abroad, in contrast, was not supposed to distinguish itself professionally and culturally by being different. On the contrary, the more it got to know the professional and cultural landscape of the host country, the better it was supposed to be able to carry out its assignment. Nevertheless, insulation from the foreign culture and social cohesiveness are, as in the case of the immigrants, useful ways of coping with a new environment. In contrast to the case of the immigrants, however, the cohesiveness and alienation that helped the foreign aid group to cope with its new environment were highly antithetical to the productive contribution that the group was expected to make. In other words, the problem of AID Americans abroad was not cliquishness *per se*, but the fact that cliquishness had counterproductive professional effects in this particular organizational setting.

The function of social cohesiveness and alienation of a foreign group extends beyond helping that group cope with the disruption and strangeness of living in a new world. Just as important, the morale of a service-oriented bureaucracy can be improved considerably when its employees are able to gripe to each other about "the beneficiary."[10] This griping serves the function of relieving employee tension and frustration arising from contact with clients, and it helps overcome competitiveness and distrust among employees by providing a focus for social cohesion. Although such griping is functional within the organization, it is *dysfunctional* with respect to the employee's relations with the beneficiary. At the same time that alienation helps improve employee morale and create social cohesiveness within the organization, it also reinforces feelings of hostility toward, or apartness from, the beneficiary and his culture. In a study of the employees of a welfare agency, Blau comments that "joking and complaining about applicants . . . immunized interviewers against experiencing such conflict [with clients] as disruptive, which *enabled them to treat clients less considerately and therefore made conflicts with clients more likely.*"[11] A perfect example of these two opposite effects of alienation to the beneficiary is the statement of a senior Foreign Service Officer about morale in the country missions. "One generally finds a better class of people at the hardship posts," he says. "That is, the same individuals tend to behave better toward each other when there is shared hardship or shared cultural apartness. There is nothing like making do with scarce supplies or exposure to local hostility to stimulate intramural comity."[12]

In short, the alienation of Americans abroad not only served to help them and their families adjust to a strange land but also played an important role in building social cohesion and relieving tension in the organization for which they worked. Needless to say, when alienation is functional in an employee's work *and* non-work world, it will be reinforced in one world because of its functionality in the other.

Social cohesiveness and alienation of a group such as U.S. government personnel abroad, then, is a perfectly predictable phenomenon. As in the case of immigrant groups, it has been a healthy way of coping with the disruption and strangeness of living in a new world. It has helped overcome the tension and competitiveness of a public sector organization requiring considerable contact with beneficiaries.

This discussion is ironic in light of the basic rationale underlying the use of country missions rather than the system used by organizations such as the IBRD and IDB, which domiciled their staff in a familiar world (Washington) from which they were sent out on periodic field missions. The country mission approach was based on the belief that development assistance involved more than routine, cut-and-dried transfers of capital, and that such efforts could be successful only if institutional and experiential factors were brought to bear on the design of development projects. This could be done only through the technician with a feel for the country, constant exposure to its problems, and familiarity with its professionals — specifically, by having the technician live in the assisted country. "I am convinced," said an Alliance for Progress administrator at a congressional hearing, "that, to the extent we do a good job, it is because we have our people in the field. . . . They really get to know the situation, know the problems, know the people, in a way which the traveling mission that comes in and looks at a project and leaves after six weeks never really can. Out of that knowledge, that background, from being present, come some pretty imaginative ideas sometimes about how to tackle some very complicated problems."[13]

There is no doubt that this unique aspect of AID structure sometimes resulted in project proposals and design features that strayed laudably from established practice, proposals which one would never have expected to emerge from the institutional environment of the Washington-based IBRD or IDB. However, the possibility that such inventiveness might have become the norm in AID was probably completely obviated by the effects of establishing an "immigrant group" abroad with the directive to merge with the society at large.

It is difficult to say which is the lesser evil: the technician residing abroad, whose work is adversely affected by the habit of social alienation through which he and his family have adjusted — or the technician based in Washington, who makes forays into the field with a briefcaseful of techniques and not much feel for the possibilities and limitations of the country he visits. One advantage of residence in the home country, at least, is that a general alienation from the culture one works in is not a functional part of one's existence.

THE ADDED INDUCEMENT TO WORK ABROAD

Much criticism has been leveled at the extra allowances, Post Exchange (PX), and other privileges that have enabled Americans abroad to live well, and conspicuously so. The privileges and allowances available to the AID employee abroad — and to a somewhat lesser extent, the State Department employee — were roughly the following: access to the Army PX; a housing allowance, in the form of a ceiling, which covered rent and utilities; APO (Army Post Office) privileges, which made it possible for employees abroad to circumvent the mail system of the host country, and to import goods duty-free from all over the world; the loan and free maintenance by AID of furniture, stove, refrigerator, air conditioner, washing machine, and dryer; the right to organize a liquor pool, whereby liquor could be purchased at approximately one-third U.S. retail price; government medical care in case of accident; one free round trip per year for each dependent enrolled in U.S. schools; and several other allowances (education, hardship, transfer, etc.) whose availability was dependent on particular circumstances.

Most of the perquisites were authorized by the Overseas Allowances and Differential Act of 1960 (ODAA), covering American government civilian personnel abroad, and Title IX of the Foreign Service Act of 1946 as amended. They were meant "to improve and strengthen the administration of overseas activities of the Government by . . . providing a means for more effectively compensating Government employees for the extra costs and hardships incident to their assignment overseas . . . [and by] facilitating for the Government the recruitment and retention of the best qualified personnel for civilian service overseas" (Sec. 101 of ODAA). A post allowance was sometimes provided "to offset the difference between the cost of living at the post of assignment to the employee in a foreign area and the cost of living in Washington, District of Columbia" (Sec. 221[1] of ODAA). The education allowance was meant to defer the cost of obtaining such elementary and secondary educational services "as are ordinarily provided without charge by the public schools in the United States" (Sec. 221[A]). The living quarters allowance, in the case where government furnished quarters were not provided, was meant to cover the costs of "rent, heat, light, fuel, gas, electricity, and water" (Sec. 211[2]). As the State Department's Task Force Study on Perquisites reported, "Living quarters abroad is, thus, an added incentive for overseas service."[14] The system of perquisites, the task force explained, was meant to "enable the employees serving overseas to enjoy, at no additional cost to themselves, the same quality of public service and amenities enjoyed by other Americans [at home]. There is no justification for the employee suffering unnecessary financial or other hardships when an adequate perquisite system could alleviate such hardship."[15]

Even if one admits that it is necessary to offer some kind of inducement to make people work abroad, it is obvious that these particular perquisites were not equivalent to a purely financial inducement. Rather, they amounted to a distinct style of living that could not be traded in, if the employee preferred another style, for cash. It is ironic that an employer would have gone about the task of seeking persons who were interested in living abroad, who got along well in foreign cultures, and who could learn the language, by holding out the promise that the new employees would be able to live just as if they were at home.

Just as ironic is the fact that this employer offered less inducement to the person who liked being abroad and living with the products of the host country culture by not allowing him to trade in the "life-style benefits" for their roughly equivalent value in cash. In 1968, an AID professional without dependents, earning $10,500 annually in Rio de Janeiro, was entitled to reimbursement for housing and utilities expenditures at a rate of $2400 a year. If he spent less, he received less. In 1974, an AID professional with two children, earning $19,500 in Quito, Ecuador, was entitled to a housing allowance of $4100. The allowances vary considerably with salary, city, and number of dependents, though these two different cases show the same proportion: the cash value of the benefit alone, if completely used, would amount to 22 percent of the salary. Adding this to the monetary value of the PX and APO privileges, as well as other allowances such as that for education, one can see that the AID perquisites represented a potential addition of much more than 22 percent to an employee's overseas salary. This increment was remarkably high, given the fact that it could not be traded in for cash by those who could not use it to its fullest or by those who preferred spending their money on something else.

The PX privilege was a good example of the contradiction inherent in the AID perquisites. The PX, after all, was an invention of the American armed forces, meant to provide for personnel stationed in an admittedly difficult environment, or at least one in which friendliness was not required for the proper execution of an assignment. The PX was meant not only to provide certain food, drug, and household items that were not available in the host country but also to compensate the serviceman for the unpleasantness of the environment in which he was obliged to serve. Hence the PX also offered nonessential items, like cameras, which helped make the serviceman's leisure hours more pleasant; likewise, the Exchange carried items that, although easily obtainable on the local market, were perhaps not of the quality to which the American was accustomed. Finally, many PX items sold at prices substantially below U.S. retail prices, let alone the prices on the local market. Hence the PX offered a substantial financial saving to those who had to buy certain items, as well as a substantial incentive to buy to those who otherwise might not have bought at all.

In contrast to the armed forces, AID officers and technicians were supposed to view the host country as an environment which one got to know and like — or, at least, understand — in the course of carrying out one's professional responsibilities. Yet the PX enabled its users to insulate themselves from an important part of the culture around them by relieving them of the need to deal with its food, its domestic appliances, its housekeeping materials, and the socializing experience that goes along with the acquisition of these items. Moreover, the availability of PX products, and their consumption-inducing prices, encouraged the American employee abroad to buy American rather than local products; it facilitated a level and quality of consumption far beyond what was possible for most local residents, in addition to being beyond the purchasing power of comparable families in the United States.

The conspicuous PX consumption of AID Americans abroad, needless to say, aroused host-country resentment and skepticism. Thus the PX ended up transforming a potentially friendly environment into a hostile one. The very fact that PX facilities were offered by the employer could not help but add to the employee's latent fear that he was starting out in an unamenable environment. On the one hand, the employer advised his new recruits profusely about the necessity, and even fun, of getting along in the host country culture; on the other, he provided comprehensive facilities for staying at arm's length from that culture and irresistible price incentives to do so. The employer's implicit admission of sympathy for those who found the local culture distasteful or uncomfortable was more effective in forming the employee's feelings toward his work environment than the panoply of orientation programs, welcome kits, informational pamphlets, and lectures which told the new AID employee and his family how to get to know, be sensitive to, and take part in the life of, the host country. It is no wonder, then, that AID Americans abroad were criticized for being clannish and insensitive to the world around them; the agency had created strong incentives to be that way.

Criticism of the PX abroad has usually focused on the "ugly American" who centered his material existence around the products of that institution. I am saying, in contrast, that the very policies of the aid organization brought out the "ugly" in the American abroad or attracted the more "ugly" of the Americans to its ranks. Locating the blame in organizational policy rather than in the American makes it possible to be a little more optimistic about the chances for improvement. It also reveals the futility of the common recommendation that the organization recruit more sensitive Americans, or saturate them with training in sensitivity once they have joined the ranks.

Another unintended consequence of the AID perquisites was that they were attractive to persons with large families. The larger the family, of course, the higher was the proportion of the breadwinner's salary required for expenditures on the AID-provided or AID-subsidized items — housing, food, toiletries, children's clothing, household appliances and materials. Indeed, one sometimes heard an AID employee say he would continue to "stay in the field" until his children were grown rather than go back to AID-Washington or another U.S.-based job, even if this meant constant uprooting and even if he didn't really like the field. (Employees assigned to Washington normally get no perquisites in addition to base salary.)

The "incentive to work abroad" of AID's special allowances and privileges, then, amounted to more of an incentive to people with certain preference patterns or family sizes. The employee who valued insulation from the culture of the host country, or who had a large family, received a higher real salary than the person who placed less value on PX products and high-standard housing, and who had a smaller family. The latter type could not cash in the unused part of his housing allowance or the amount of PX spending or APO ordering he did not do.[16] Family size, of course, was not relevant to the agency's needs. The preference patterns, however, were precisely those which the agency did not need or want, and which it tried in its orientation programs to modify.

There was one principal administrative reason for AID to favor the provision of PX facilities, housing compounds, furniture, and appliances: cost economies that could be achieved by the combined use of facilities abroad by military, AID, Foreign Service, and USIA personnel. Allowing PX privileges might conceivably have cost the agency less than supplying salary supplements for buying food on the local market; maintaining housing compounds might have cost less in some posts than providing salary supplements to cover high local housing costs; purchasing and loaning furniture and appliances cost less than financing the shipping abroad of an employee's household effects. In some countries, the arrival of AID missions on the scene in the early nineteen-sixties brought these economies of scale into effect. The number of AID personnel at a new or expanded mission often outnumbered American government personnel already located at a particular post.[17] These expenditure economies, however, were probably outweighed by the costs to the organization of attracting and retaining a less suitable type of staff member and of generating hostility in the host country.

After all the criticism of AID and all the recommendations for improvement, it is remarkable that the agency was not taken to task for paying less, in real terms, to its adventurous and adaptive technicians than to its security-seeking, foreigner-avoiding ones. The Task Force Study on Perquisites cited above, for example, did not touch on any of the considerations discussed here. Indeed, the "most controversial and emotionally significant [issue] that the Task Force undertook to study" was that having to do with the sale of personal automobiles at a profit by U.S. government employees overseas.[18]

The perquisite system was one of those rare problem situations where an obvious and easy alternative existed: providing the added inducement to work abroad in purely monetary form. In fact, monetary inducement is already used by the agency, in the form of a "post differential" for some cities. The post differential is a percentage increment to salary that is granted when certain aspects of life at the post are considered difficult; in Guayaquil, Ecuador, for example, the post differential is 20 percent. Thus the concept of a purely monetary inducement for AID employees is not new, although its coexistence with the other perquisites described above results in an inducement system that is not monetary.

CONCLUSION

Although the foreign aid agency was well-matched in some ways with its task environment, some aspects of its performance revealed a serious mismatching.[19] The newness of its task and the uncertainty of its task environment were best handled by a decentralized organization with less formal procedures, substantial points of contact with the environment, the possession of discretionary power by those having such contact, and an ability on their part to influence policy and improve their position in the organization. As shown above, AID seemed to have all this. But decentralization across national boundaries brought with it the undesirable result of making alienation from the environment a functional aspect of organizational life. The agency itself, of course, added to the problem by resorting to a system of perquisites that reinforced tendencies toward alienation.

The need for a large beneficiary input, along with the uncharted nature of the task, made desirable and possible the possession of considerable discretion by the far-flung agents of the organization. Like decentralization, however, discretion in this setting had its drawbacks. The discretion-holding members of the organization were, by virtue of rank and geographic location, the type of bureau officials least likely to adapt and innovate. Again, the problem was exacerbated by the perverse incentives of the perquisite system.

A multilateralized, donor-country-based institution — staffed with well-recruited and well-trained technicians — would not necessarily do away with the dilemmas of decentralization and discretion. The IBRD exemplifies this sort of institution, but its professionals have been no less subject to criticism than those of AID for adherence to traditional thinking.[20] Among development assistance organizations, however, the IBRD is considered the best in engineering and economic analysis of projects. Perhaps its location in the developed world has much to do with this particular combination of narrowness and excellence. In this developed-world setting, away from the task environment, the professional receives more respect, rewards, and support for being good at applying existing techniques of problem-solving. As has been seen above, however, such techniques do not necessarily generate learning about new ways of doing things. Thus while organizational location in the developed world may be necessary for bringing together and maintaining a certain kind of professional competence, it has an important drawback. Such location may make the acquisition of the requisite organizational skills difficult, because it almost eliminates intellectual tension with the task environment.

Chapter Four

THE INSTITUTIONALIZATION
OF OUTSIDE CRITICISM

It is well known that, from the start, the U.S. foreign aid program was subjected to constant criticism, expressed in congressional hearings and investigations, GAO audits, muckraking journalism, and claims by various other government departments that their programs or interests were being jeopardized by the foreign aid program. Foreign aid has also been vigorously attacked by its sympathizers, but I am interested here in exploring the effects of the major part of the criticism: that which stemmed from the unpopularity of foreign aid.

The excessive amount of critical attention focused on the program has various explanations. Foreign aid was never popular with the American public; its proponents made unrealistic claims about what could be accomplished in order to push it through Congress; and it was politically safe for a politician to criticize the program, since none of its activities lay in the constituencies of colleague politicians. The program's unpopularity resulted in a series of executive restrictions and amendments to the foreign assistance legislation which limited considerably the agency's room for maneuver, and were often contrary to the program's goals.[1] These constraints, along with a lack of strong executive support for the agency, created a kind of year-round open season on the agency for other government agencies acting in their own interests or expressing the wishes of private interest groups.

The agency's vulnerability to such incursions was increased by the

38

fact that it, unlike domestic money-spending bureaucracies, had no constituency. American equipment suppliers, for example, were not the constituency one would expect them to be. They did not appear among those outside interest groups who supported the foreign aid bill when it was annually reviewed by the Congress. Though U.S. equipment sales to AID-financed projects were publicized by the agency in the localities where the equipment was manufactured, this was more a defense against accusations that foreign aid drains U.S. dollars away from American goods than the reporting back to a faithful constituent. When the Senate voted down the foreign aid bill for the first time in history, in 1971, The *Wall Street Journal* carried an article entitled "U.S. Firms Push to Get Aid Bill Resurrected" (November 3). The article turned out, however, to be a description of the companies and equipment that had received AID financing in the past, and it seemed to be based on an agency information release. The title of the article, then, may have been closer to wishful thinking than fact.[2]

AID's beneficiaries — the aid-receiving countries — were outside the American political system, and hence could not be drawn upon for the politicking necessary to gain congressional support or for the hell-raising necessary to prevent threatened appropriations cuts. This meant, in turn, that the program was unusually dependent on a substantial investment of the executive's power and prestige.[3] This type of executive support was chronically absent, as noted above, so that the foreign aid program had neither the normal beneficiary source of support nor the executive backing to compensate for that deficiency. Finally, the constant criticism of AID, and the latter's vulnerability, made it very difficult for the agency to carry out its task. In 1970, the AID Administrator reported that he had been surprised by two things after getting to know his organization. One was "the fact that we have as many good people as we have," and the second was his discovery of "an agency that is so largely oriented toward defending itself against critics."[4]

The unpopularity of foreign aid and the impact of this unpopularity on organizational performance were recognized to some extent in the official evaluations of the program. Thus some of the recommendations for change were aimed at insulating the organization from the effects of this unpopularity. The proposals for multilateralization and for converting the aid agency into a bank, for example, were based on an explicit recognition of the entity's vulnerability to successful attack by other arms of government.[5] Less explicitly, they were meant to counteract the weakness caused by a chronic absence of strong executive support during those times when the organization had to do battle with other government entities.

It has been generally recognized that criticism of the foreign aid program weakened the agency and kept it from doing what it wanted to do. Less understood is the fact that the process of living with criticism profoundly affected what the agency *wanted* to do and what it was capable of doing. Although official and other evaluations of foreign aid have sometimes admitted to the debilitating effects of criticism, they do not trace its institutionalization to the point where one can see that such criticism accounts in part for faulty performance. Before elaborating, I would like to make a few additional observations about the nature of the criticism and the reasons for it.

AUDITING THE UNKNOWN, AND BAD BENEFICIARY FEEDBACK

AID had the same problems as any federal bureaucracy with money to spend: the pressure to commit resources; the use of project analysis to rationalize decisions already taken rather than to arrive at decisions; the drumming up of business (i.e., the creation of projects) by departments anxious to keep themselves in existence; and a risk-averse behavior caused partly by the conspicuousness of mistakes and the less visible, less well-defined standards of success. Such money-spending bureaucracies are supposed to be kept in check by the independent eyes of watchdog groups like congressional investigating committees, the General Accounting Office, and the Office of Management and the Budget. This system of checks is considered a healthy and necessary counterbalance to a government agency's natural inclination to spend for the sake of spending, to pursue project mixes out of joint with the national interest or its own declared goals, or to place first priority on justifying the existence of the organization. Although the system of checks may have been criticized in some instances for opening the door to undesirable political influences, or for its harmful sniping by audit-minded evaluators who do not understand the substance of a program, the principle of the system has been generally accepted as necessary to a well-functioning public sector.

The nature of the task of a bureaucracy that spends money outside the country is so different from that of its domestic counterparts that control of it may be quite difficult within the system generally applied to home-based public agencies. The incipient state of knowledge about the development process and development assistance techniques — compared to the more advanced development of knowledge and standards concerning problems confronted by home bureaucracies — means that there are few clear conceptions of what is right, what is wrong, and what is inconsistent with the foreign aid entity's declared goals. Hence the technique of watchdogging a development program is, in a certain sense, just as underdeveloped as the knowledge about how to help countries develop.[6] Yet the same auditors, evaluators, and investigators who check the activities of the home bureaucracies are enlisted to check those of the foreign-spending bureaucracy, using the same criteria of judgment and evaluation that have been developed through their domestic experience. Thus the foreign aid program is often subject to irrelevant and harmful criticism and, perhaps more important, frequently does not receive criticism and control in areas where it is, in fact, making mistakes.

The distant location of the foreign aid bureaucracy's constituency and projects removes the scene of action from the watchdog entities' world of experience. They do not have a feel for this other world they must check up on, and hence have a hard time judging what is an acceptable degree of failure, what is an inevitable and unimportant type of problem, what is a reasonable explanation of a problem and what is devious, what raises suspicions and what does not — the kind of feel that helps guide these investigators through their work on the home bureaucracies.

The watchdogs seem to compensate for their lack of familiarity with the world in which foreign aid projects are built by making a stricter and more comprehensive application of routine check-and-balance criteria — as if to make up for the loss of one sense faculty by the increased use of another. This increased rigorousness, of course, only emphasizes the inapplicability of such criteria to areas outside the domain for which the criteria were devised. The agency, in turn, balked at the "unrealistic performance and implementation standards" imposed not only by the GAO, the congressional internal inspection staff, the inspector general of the AID program process, and the Office of Management and the Budget, but by the agency's own auditors. "Application of U.S. construction and performance standards to less orderly under-developed country setting[s]," the agency complained to Congress, "creates considerable country friction, discourages innovation and penalizes justifiable risk-taking by AID; [it] holds the Agency to a publicly damaging standard of accountability."[7]

Another reason the agency was vulnerable to sniping by the watchdog entities relates to the unusually large share of its work that was contributed by its beneficiary, the recipient-country borrower institution. The recipient was partially responsible for designing the projects to be financed, mobilizing local political support for budgetary appropriations for local currency costs, and providing the local institutional overhead, professional capacity, and sheer will that was essential for carrying out a project. Hence the aid organization was extremely dependent on the public it served, but that public was both institutionally and politically outside its control. At the same time, however, the agency was held completely accountable by the watchdog entities for the quality of its output, even though such a large portion of that quality was beyond its control. When the agency tried to explain a problem as the result of the failure of the recipient country to do its share, the watchdog entity would tend to dismiss the response as excuse-making.

For a money-spending bureaucracy operating outside the country, in sum, the checks and balances of watchdog entities came into play in a peculiarly counterproductive way. AID, inherently vulnerable to harsh criticism, became more and more preoccupied with protecting itself from the watchdogs, retreating under the safe cover of close adherence to standard procedures, and fearing the exposure that might result from risk-taking and experiment.

The agency was also vulnerable because it served as a target — in a way that the State Department never could — for criticism of United States foreign policy. Wherever large amounts of money are being spent, there will be an unavoidable minimum of misspending, inefficiency, and graft. The number of possible mistakes in a program like AID's, therefore, will be much greater than in the State Department, simply because the latter does not have to build projects and rely on outsiders for essential inputs. The State Department, under criticism, could at least attempt to close ranks. AID, in contrast, was exposed on all sides: the objects on which it had spent money were out in the open for anyone who wanted to see, and persons outside the agency who had worked on its projects were around for questioning. The undertaking by the U.S. government of a large foreign aid program in the nineteen-sixties, then, brought on to the political scene a more tangible target than the State Department for the rising dissatisfaction with U.S. foreign policy.

As noted above, AID, unlike domestic bureaucracies, had no domestic constituents on whom it could count for political support. This meant that the agency was deprived of an important source of criticism and received in its place a type of criticism which was useless in the organization's internal efforts to promote change and innovation. That is, when the foreign aid beneficiary felt that AID was giving him short shrift, he muttered under his breath and toed the line instead of "writing to his Congressman," telling the newspapers, organizing action groups, or seeking alliances with sympathetic groups inside the bureaucracy. He accepted something unacceptable as the price of getting foreign assistance, and grumbled resentfully. The agency was deprived, in other words, of constructive negative feedback from its beneficiaries because they were outside the political system. Just as important, the innovating technician in AID could not rely on beneficiary feedback to help him argue the case for change *within* the confines of his own organization. AID, therefore, had the worst of both worlds in relation to beneficiary feedback: it was severely and publicly criticized by the beneficiary and at the same time was not able to enlist these critics as allies in attempts to bring about internal change. Already criticism-prone by nature, the foreign aid organization received its beneficiary criticism in a form that was not usable.[8]

THE INCURSIONS

Foreign assistance legislation placed a series of constraints on AID action in the name of protecting certain private or public U.S. interests. Although the harmfulness of this type of constraint has been recognized, as mentioned above, little attention has been paid to the institutional form it took and how it affected the agency's work, independent of the specific content of the constraint. The government entity charged with policing the legislative constraint frequently ended up having a power over the organization considerably greater than the original constraint intended — a power that spread into areas where the policing agency may have had no authority or experience.

The constraint itself, then, posed one type of problem for the agency; an almost completely independent problem was the power over AID gained by the policing entity in the form of its (the former's) daily presence — actual, expected, or feared — on the agency's work scene.

Although interbureaucratic struggle and attempted incursions by one public sector agency into the territory of another are typical, we have seen that the foreign aid agency was peculiarly unequipped for such struggle. As a result, it too often gave in to the desires of the other entity or altered its decisions to avoid expected incursions. Needless to say, this brought on even more bullying from the outside. An example from the Treasury Department illustrates the point. I take the example from the Treasury rather than the Commerce Department or the Congress, because considerable attention has already been paid to the disruptive effects of the pressures of private interest groups exerted on AID through the latter two. The Treasury, in contrast, was charged with protecting the public rather than the private interest, i.e., policing activities in any sector which were thought to have an adverse effect on the balance of payments. Constraints imposed by the Treasury in the name of protecting the U.S. balance of payments, for example, came down hard on private business interests as well as on AID.[9] The Treasury as example, then, illustrates how AID was undermined by institutional forces within the very government that created it — independently of the more widely criticized pressures of private interest groups.

The Treasury, along with the Budget Bureau, had what amounted to veto power over all AID projects. This power was based partially on administrative procedure established by President Johnson in 1965, whereby the president, on advice of the Treasury and Bureau of the Budget, was required to approve all AID projects over $5 million (this amount was later changed to $10 million). Moreover, AID was supposed to consult with the Treasury, the Commerce Department, the Export-Import Bank, and the State Department before approving any project, through meetings of the interagency Development Loan Committee (provided for in Section 204 of the Foreign Assistance Act of 1961 as amended). Although the statutory directive to consult with the Treasury and other departments did not confer formal veto power on them, the practice of AID administrators in recent years has been to arrive at a consensus with these departments before approving a project. In reality, then, the Treasury had veto power over all AID project proposals. Its authority was based on, among other things, its responsibility for the U.S. balance of payments. It watched over the amount of local-cost financing in a proposed AID loan in order to see that there was no more of such financing than was allowed by law, or than was absolutely necessary. Local costs, unlike dollar costs tied to purchases of U.S. exports, were considered to result in a net outflow of U.S. dollars.[10] (Since 1970, the strictures on local-cost financing have been relaxed somewhat, as discussed in chapter 6.)

The Treasury held considerable discretion in the exercise of its responsibilities because the severity of balance of payments problems varied and the conditions under which local-cost financing was permissible left considerable room for interpretation. In the process of evaluating a proposed project including local-cost financing, therefore, the Treasury might have objected to the project on the grounds that it was not "a good project" and hence was unworthy of the local-cost financing which, on purely procedural grounds, might have been justified. For example, the Treasury threatened for several weeks to veto an agricultural project involving the AID guarantee of financed sales of land to peasants because it considered the project "politically risky." This type of judgment, of course, falls within the purview of the State Department, if not AID itself. The State Department, however, had not considered it necessary to exercise its veto power in this case, and had already approved the project. Although the Treasury grudgingly approved the project in the end, after several weeks of the informal telephone bargaining that often precedes the meeting at which votes are taken, it nonetheless did so with the admonition that AID had "better not do something like that again." Needless to say, the Treasury had neither the authority nor the experience to decide on such a question.

Another example of bureaucratic intrusion relates to the much-criticized "additionality" procedures, which were watched over by the Treasury and Commerce departments. The procedures, dating from 1964, were part of the program to alleviate the U.S. balance of payments deficit. Additionality sought to go beyond the concept of tied aid by requiring that U.S. aid financing result in recipient-country imports from the U.S. above and beyond what would have been imported through normal commercial channels, without aid. The procedures included special provisions written into a number of loan agreements requiring that funds be used only for imports in excess of the recipient country's normal marketing requirements (e.g., fertilizer), the inclusion of U.S. export promotion as an explicit criterion for selecting capital projects and commodities for AID financing, the favoring of capital projects with potential for follow-up orders, and the use of "negative" and "positive" lists. In 1967, AID started using positive lists, which limited commodities that could be imported under AID program loans to specific categories. "For the most part," testified AID Administrator Gaud to the Congress, "positive lists are made up of commodities in which the United States is relatively less competitive, and which we would otherwise be unlikely to export in any great volume. . . . All of these efforts [to ensure additionality] except the removal of discriminatory barriers are restrictions on the operation of free market forces."[11]

Additionality was resented and criticized within AID. It required the imposition of restrictive procedures on recipient-country import systems. It put AID in the embarrassing position of encouraging freer trade practices in the recipient country on general economic grounds while simultaneously enforcing additionality procedures which amounted to a protection of those American industries least competitive in world trade.[12] It complicated and slowed down the disbursement of funds. A great deal of AID time was required to comply with the Treasury's demands that the agency prove that "additional" imports had actually occurred, that measures were being taken to increase such imports, or that AID-financed U.S. imports had not taken the place of normal quantities of nonfinanced U.S. imports.

Although AID complained for years about the incursions of the Treasury and Commerce departments in this area, it was not until the additionality story was made public and pressure applied by *outside* sources that relief came — and it came almost immediately. A highly critical article on the subject appeared in the *New York Times*,[13] the president of Colombia complained personally to the president of the United States,[14] and twenty-one Latin American nations together condemned the procedures in a report presented publicly to the American president by the foreign minister of Chile.[15] Immediately, a presidential directive ordered that additionality procedures be dropped. The move was announced publicly as a significant concession by the United States at the annual meeting of the Inter-American Economic and Social Council in Trinidad in June of 1969. "We wish to reduce to the extent possible," Secretary Meyer said, "requirements and practices extraneous to development which can impair the quality of our assistance. In this regard, the President has authorized me to say that effective immediately the present practice of applying so-called 'additionality' requirements to U.S. aid will be discontinued."[16] Notwithstanding this ceremonious and high level approach to the end of additionality, AID missions received instructions from headquarters a few months later that they had been advised by the Treasury that it would continue "to take additionality considerations into account" in decisions concerning the approval of projects.

In sum, a significant and long-fought-for presidential directive seeking to protect the foreign aid program would be transgressed in day-to-day operations. This was the simple result of the bureaucratic power over AID that had been gained by the Treasury in the exercise of its mandate to protect the U.S. balance of payments. AID had to "live with" the Treasury, as well as the other government departments with watchdog mandates, regardless of the scope of the specific directives that entitled the other agencies to authority over AID.[17]

LIVING WITH CRITICISM

Criticism and intrusion affected the agency's performance by changing the AID technician's concept of what he wanted to do. One of the best ways to illustrate this result of living with other government agencies is to cite the text of an unclassified AID memo concerning a proposed loan. In arguing the case for a proposed $29.4 million loan for long-distance microwave equipment, the country mission in Brazil pointed out that the loan would result in major purchases of U.S. equipment. These purchases would otherwise have not taken place, it was argued, because the American equipment was 10 to 20 percent higher in cost than that of European or Japanese suppliers.

The Mission drew EMBRATEL's and the GOB's [Government of Brazil] attention to the fact that AID financing terms would more than offset the price disadvantage on the basis of present value comparisons with the shorter European credits . . . . Because of the higher price of the U.S. equipment and the lack of adequate export financing, U.S. suppliers would not be competitive without the proposed AID loan. Also, telecommunications sales engender repeat orders because of the need to standardize on a few types of equipment. Thus, this loan would significantly serve the commercial interests of the U.S. by increasing exports of this equipment in the future.[18]

In short, the concessional terms of the loan would compensate for the higher cost of the American equipment; and, in the bargain, the Brazilians decided at a later date to buy the equipment from the Japanese, partly because of the better prices.

The notable aspect of this document in terms of the discussion here is not that a statement was made identifying the foreign aid program explicitly with U.S. business interests, but that the passage quoted was not given some kind of confidential classification. The writers of the statement did not think it necessary to conceal this consideration, express it in veiled language, or classify it. After all, the statement was a perfect piece of "evidence" for critics who considered the aid program a U.S. export subsidy in disguise and thought that foreign aid technicians were working hand in hand with U.S. business groups.

Such "collusion" is usually expected to take the form of behind-doors conversations and agreements never committed to paper, certainly not unclassified paper. Yet, this type of statement exists in one of many such documents available to the public, revealing goals that are directly contrary to the aims of the aid program. It is ironic that those who criticize U.S. foreign aid as an arm of U.S. imperialism have relied on infrequently leaked confidential documents or exposés of ex-officials in order to document their accusations, when so much "evidence" exists in more easily obtainable form.[19]

How can one explain the openness of such a statement, given the agency's hypersensitivity to criticism, its fear of the written word, and the corresponding tendency to "overclassify" what it wrote? The answer is quite simple. To the AID bureaucrat's eyes, the cited statement served the purpose of warding off criticism rather than bringing it down on the agency's head. It was not a case of collusion with U.S. business, but of pleasing the Treasury on balance-of-payments grounds and the Department of Commerce on export-promotion grounds. Concern over the Treasury and the Department of Commerce, in sum, blacked out the ability of the drafters to perceive their own organization's goals. This uncharacteristic absence of protective concern is perhaps best explained by concluding that the one thing the agency did not have to worry about was the accusation that it was subverting its own goals. Despite all the criticism heaped upon the Agency, criticism of this particular type was rare. Or, more accurately, although this type of criticism had been directed at the foreign aid program from various quarters for some time, it was never the cause of real or threatened reductions in appropriations,[20] of meddling incursions by other government agencies, or threatened vetoes of project proposals by the Treasury, State Department, Commerce Department, and Export-Import Bank. Although this type of criticism existed, it came from sources outside the context of the agency's bureaucratic struggle to survive — i.e., from the recipient countries, the academic community, and, most strenuously yet least known to foreign aid critics, from within the agency itself.

The criticism of AID emanating from other government entities singled out various factors. GAO audit reports, congressional inquiries, hearings, and debates on appropriations chronicled items such as inefficiency, lack of proper auditing, misspending of funds, incompetence, hostile or other unappreciative behavior by recipient countries, aggravation of U.S. balance of payments problems, decreases in the U.S. export share of aided country markets, and damage to specific U.S. business groups. AID, in short, was never called on the carpet by these entities for designing projects that were optimal for American interests and suboptimal or economically irrational for the countries being assisted in their economic development.

The quoted document, then, shows how AID institutionalized its toleration of criticism by coming to identify with the very interests of the bureaucratic entities which it was trying to fend off. One might say that the agency experienced a strange case of "displacement of goals." Goal displacement usually refers to the substitution of ends by means; for example, an organization's procedures may be observed so strictly that its stated goals are defeated. In the case of AID, what does the displacing is not the agency's own means, converted into ends, but the goals that belong to outside entities with interests counter to the agency's. The calculated attention paid by the agency to the goals of others can, of course, be interpreted as the means to an end: conforming to the Treasury's interests, for example, would help the agency make loans. But I am talking about something different — namely, the uncalculated, unrecognized replacement of goals by contradictory ones. This is carried to the point where the bureaucrat, as in the case cited above, no longer knows that he is transgressing his organization's original goals and comes to identify easily with the alien ones.

There was a significant difference, then, between the specific legal constraints placed on the agency's action and the institutional form these constraints took. The AID bureaucrat unknowingly came to serve other masters. This explains, in part, the lack of innovative and adaptive behavior in the agency. It was not merely a case of wanting to be adaptive and innovative and feeling oneself constrained from doing so. Often, one simply did not want to adapt — or even think of adapting — because one's goals had become attached to concerns other than economic development. The organization's goals, in sum, had been overcome by the struggle to survive in a hostile environment.[21]

The Written Word

In AID, as in many bureaucracies, one was urged or required to put many things "in writing." Moreover, if one held a minority position on a particular issue, one's stand would sometimes be recognized as a force to be contended with only if it were committed to official paper. Even the dissent of a low-ranking technician would suddenly take on importance after being put in writing and distributed liberally within the organization. Official meetings would be called to recognize and discuss the technician's dissent, and considerable effort would be made, if he were not conceded to, to bring him to a compromise position.

Because of AID's vulnerability to outside attack, this power of the written word was to some extent based on the fear of it. If the most powerless of technicians raised a problem in writing, then the person responsible, no matter how high his position, considered it essential to produce a satisfactory response in writing. If not, he considered himself a sitting duck for the future congressional or GAO file prober who discovered the problem-raising memo in the file without a satisfactory reply sitting behind it.

Sometimes the mere writing of a reply would be enough, bureaucratically, to contend with the issue. There would be no verbal confrontation between disagreeing parties, no grappling with the issue, and no attempt to come to agreement. The problem would be put to rest in the file by putting the response in with it, as if the dissenter had never existed in real life. This might happen when the dissent, or the dissenter, did not have enough supporters in positions of power. The power of the written word in these instances was its overcoming of dissent by deflecting it into channels where it could be disposed of. In such cases, the written word drained the dissenter of power, since he had entered a game in which it would be easy for the other side to claim a false victory.

At other times, the act of writing had a catalytic effect, bringing about verbal confrontations and grappling with issues. This usually happened when the written dissent, which had previously gone unheeded, attracted the interest of otherwise uninvolved superiors. In this case, the written word conferred real power on the dissenter. Writing was important, then, not only because it was required, but because it could be an instrument for gaining recognition and leverage. Writing was of special importance to the agency, moreover, because of the newness of the task and the corresponding lack of a literature on how to go about it.

Although the dissenting AID technician valued the written word as an instrument for being heard, he had, at the same time, a considerable fear of it. His fear was based on the repercussions that his writing might evoke from superiors. For writing what he considered a straightforward description of a problem or a balanced evaluation of a project, an AID technician might be remonstrated with, "What would Congress or the GAO say if they got hold of that!?" The technician himself, moreover, had been made aware of the real and expected critical scrutiny of AID by other government entities. He knew of the possible harmful repercussions on the organization that his openness might cause, in the form of reprimands, more constraining directives, an ensuing decrease of flexibility, and ultimately, the specter of increased public hostility leading to reduced appropriations. In trying to put description or dissent down on paper, the AID technician knew that his writing, if not careful, might someday be used by an outsider to betray his agency.

The AID technician, then, sat before the typewriter with a sense of the power of his words and his responsibility for articulating his ideas, along with a tremendous fear of his own writing. When he wanted to make a written contribution, he was constrained by the feeling that he might be betraying his organization or the people around him. Words were toned down, thoughts were twisted, and arguments were left out, all in order to alleviate the uncomfortable feeling of responsibility for possible betrayal. The writing was finished with a sense of frustration at not having articulated an argument as lucidly, honestly, and convincingly as possible. Such a situation must have resulted in a certain atrophy of the capacity for written communication — and, inevitably, for all communication through language.[22]

The writing problems described here are characteristic, to some extent, of most public bureaucracies. AID was different, however, because the geographical distance between headquarters and the field, as well as between field offices themselves, made the written word necessary for communication. Writing was necessary, in short, for the actual relating of things, in addition to its standard bureaucratic function of recording verbal agreements. At the same time, however, writing was riskier in AID because of the excessive vulnerability of the agency to criticism.

The nature of the writing problem in AID and the reasons for it can be better understood by comparing it to the writing of the State Department's Foreign Service Officers in the field. Foreign Service writing was also characterized by forced restraint and veiled language. Feared repercussion was due in this case to inaccurate analysis or prediction, or too-strongly worded disagreement. A flair for writing was nevertheless considered a valuable talent in the Foreign Service. Much of the officer's work, after all, amounted to journalism — reporting the unfolding of political events, describing the personality of an unpredictable politician, conveying the atmosphere of a tense scene of conflict. A young officer's narrative talent would often be approvingly noted by his colleagues, and such facility at writing could be a factor in promotion.[23] Writing was a much more functional part of the Foreign Service Officer's job than it was for the AID employee.

These differing attitudes toward writing were a result of the differing functions of written communication in the two agencies. In the Foreign Service, especially at lower levels, one wrote as a dispassionate observer of a strange and unpredictable world. Even if it did not bear on a current policy decision, the well-written account was commended. In the AID mission, in contrast, one took to the typewriter not to describe the world outside but to bring considerations to bear on decisions in one's own organization. One discussed what the organization and its projects were doing, and what they had done in the past. AID writing, in short, was much more self-involved than writing in the State Department, where one did not have to worry that the people being described would ever read what was written about them or their country. In AID writing, one rarely saw the lingering descriptions, the amused disdain, or the adjectival abundance characteristic of Foreign Service reports. The AID technician was writing about the doings of himself, his colleagues, and his superiors.

As a consequence of these differences, State Department files contain a rich chronicling of political events as they unfold in important and unimportant places abroad. In AID, in contrast, there is a paucity of good reports on the valuable development experiences lived through by the organization's personnel. Ironically, the State Department is often said to overdo the chronicling of events, in relation to its need for such input in decisionmaking.[24] The foreign aid program, in contrast, had a profound need, which it could not fulfill, for inside writing about what it did.

Chapter Five

THE ABUNDANCE
OF DEVELOPMENT ASSISTANCE

It appears to anyone who has spent much time in a development assistance organization that people are making decisions as if aid funds were abundant. How can this be, when everyone else knows how truly scarce development assistance is? How can this happen, when the borrower country is constantly facing problems caused by foreign exchange and capital scarcity? — when one of the major reasons that lenders are on the scene is to alleviate problems caused by this kind of scarcity? — when lending institutions have made painstaking attempts to prevent this from happening? Are donor organizations simply promoting their own growth, in Parkinsonian fashion, appealing to conscience-arousing arguments in order to squeeze more money for themselves out of their sponsors?

The answer to these questions lies in the organizational factors described in this and the following two chapters. Aid scarcity and abundance *both* exist, if one defines each with respect to different contexts. The more familiar scarcity of development assistance refers to aggregate amounts of resources required and supplied — a scarcity expressed in the well-known estimates of foreign exchange or savings "gaps"; in the calculations of development assistance as a percentage of the donor country's national product; and in the target growth rates proposed as necessary for recipient countries to achieve "self-sustaining growth," which are rates that require a certain level of outside assistance.

54

The less conspicuous "abundance," in contrast, refers to the institutional environment in which the capital transfer takes place. As will be shown below, the donor agencies have certain goals, procedures, and standards of performance as organizations which inadvertently contribute to a tacit conception of the supply of development assistance funds as unlimited. Given the real scarcity of development assistance in aggregate terms, this organizational ambience of abundance results in a highly inefficient allocation of resources.

My purpose in drawing the distinction between aggregate scarcity and organizational abundance is not simply to show that organizations are worlds unto themselves, whose actions may or may not be related to the goals they are supposed to be serving. Rather, I want to show how the "inside" conception of development assistance as abundant evolved while the rest of the world was perceiving it as scarce; how this conception has adversely affected the performance of donor organizations; and how it has contributed significantly to problems which are usually traced to other causes.

The "abundance problem" has two different causes, which reinforce each other substantially: the limitation of financing to mainly the foreign-exchange or import costs of projects, and the pressure on donor organizations to lend all the resources they can command. The financing of mainly import costs is a policy problem, and hence of more obvious resolution. The organizational problem is more in the nature of a bureaucratic phenomenon which is difficult to modify and might require radical change in the institutional form of development assistance. The aid recipient, strangely enough, also participates in the perception of assistance as abundant, and thus contributes inadvertently to the problem performance of donor organizations.

One of the most well known of the policy constraints placed on AID's actions was that requiring the agency to finance only the foreign exchange or import costs of a project. This policy has received much attention and criticism, and as a result it has been modified to a certain extent (see chapter 6 for a discusson of this question). It has received part of the blame for overly large projects and their correspondingly high equipment or import components. Whether or not the policy will be modified even more in the future, it has at least been sighted as a problem-causer and given its share of the blame for bad performance.

It is surprising to discover that as this particular policy has been changing, the tendency toward large import-intensive projects seems to have continued unabated. Moreover, the tendency is as strong — if not stronger — in multilateral organizations like the World Bank. This leads one to suspect that the policy constraints of the U.S. program may not be the proper culprit in this particular problem. Since the same outcome occurs in organizations living with policy constraints quite different from the bilateral AID, and since the problem persists despite the modification of the policy, one suspects that the policy of financing import costs might not account on its own for the strength of the bias toward large capital projects.

The problems caused by the policy of financing import costs have already been chronicled in the literature of foreign development assistance: there is a tendency for both donor and recipient to gravitate toward projects with high foreign exchange components, or large projects whose foreign exchange component may be small as a percentage but is large in absolute value, or project designs that require more imported equipment than others, or to encourage the importation of equipment that could be made in the recipient country.[1] In short, foreign exchange items are selected over local currency items as if the former were less scarce.

This result occurs in conjunction with a less obvious and less remarked upon bureaucratic phenomenon that favors large projects over small ones. The output of this particular type of public sector organization, that is, seems to have been defined in terms of the total amount of resources successfully transferred during any period; input is the staff work, measured in time, necessary to transfer a given amount. If one is financing projects, the staff input on any particular project will obviously not increase proportionately with the amount of money to be lent, for there are organizational economies of scale in the size of the financing. A larger project requires less staff time per dollar transferred than a smaller one, so there is a tendency for the financing organization to gravitate toward larger projects.[2] This tendency exists, moreover, even in organizations not under the pressure of an annual appropriations funding mechanism — i.e., the need to "get rid of the money" before the end of a fiscal year. The phenomenon is just as characteristic and problematic in the multilateral or bank-type lending institutions so frequently proposed as a better substitute for U.S. bilateral lending.

The definition of organizational output in terms of resources transferred may be seen as one source of the problem, since it can cause a quantity-at-any-cost approach to the task at hand. Yet that is precisely the way the task is defined in the development assistance business, a point I return to later. Suffice it to say here that this conception of output pervades the standards of procedure, the incentive system, the career motivations, and the work environment of the foreign assistance entity. Part of the problem, of course, is a result of traits that are found in many public sector bureaucracies. Just as substantial a part is unique to the foreign assistance organization.

Analysts of development assistance have recognized to a certain extent the problem of organizational economies of scale in project lending and the resulting slowness in resource flow and bias toward larger projects. To deal with the problem, they have recommended a streamlining of procedures or, less commonly, a partial or complete abandonment of the project mechanism in favor of "program loans." These are large loans for general commodity imports, based on a negotiated agreement with the recipient country as to the steps it will take in fiscal and monetary policy; they require close monitoring by the donor of the recipient's performance in these areas. Both the program loan mechanism and the recommendations for streamlining the project lending mechanism can be seen as attempts to overcome the slowness of the present resource flow.[3] The measures are not usually defended on these grounds, however, nor are they always proposed as a response to this particular problem. Program lending, for example, is usually presented as a more integrated and comprehensive "planning" approach to development assistance and economic development than the "hit-or-miss" project system.[4] Streamlined procedures are usually proposed as solutions to problems of recipient-country irritation, bureaucratic red tape, oversophisticated technical choices, and inadequately sensitive technicians.

Although these latter factors are no doubt problematical in their own right, the particular phenomenon I am discussing has been left somewhat in the shadows. That is, although the problems caused by the organizational economy of large projects and by the financing of mainly import costs have each been recognized separately, it has never been shown how the combination of the two has pervaded the environment of the donor and borrower organization. Before discussing this question at greater length, it is important to stop here and describe more precisely the decisionmaking that makes development assistance funds look abundant and leads to large projects with large import components. The following section provides some detailed examples of this kind of decisionmaking. Chapter 6 shows how the policy of financing mainly import costs contributes to the perception of abundance, particularly in the borrower; and chapter 7 examines the organizational phenomena which contribute to that perception in the lending institution.

ABUNDANCE IN ACTION: SOME EXAMPLES

The type of organizational behavior I want to illustrate is quite elusive. Development assistance institutions do not deliberately pursue import-maximization policies or favor large projects. To the contrary, they carefully screen proposed projects to make sure that the design is most efficient under given conditions. Moreover, when deciding to finance a specific project, they often require or encourage the borrower country to undertake general policy measures that will limit its foreign exchange requirements or stimulate local production. Similarly, borrowers do not devise public investment programs that purposely maximize foreign exchange components and large projects, nor do they deliberately pass up local producers to import the aid-financed good. The mechanism I want to illustrate, rather, operates almost invisibly in both lender and borrower, influencing innumerable decisions concerning factor proportions, where to buy, what to buy, what to build, how big to build it, and when. Hence it is necessary to descend to the level of small decisionmaking, of subordinates rather than superiors, in order to discover the workings of the mechanism and to understand the problems it causes.

The Turbine-Generator Story

In 1967, a state-owned power company in southern Brazil approached the AID mission in Rio de Janeiro about financing for a 250-megawatt, $110 million hydroelectric power plant, Passo Real. The installation of four 63-megawatt units was to be staggered over seven years in accordance with demand projections, the last two units constituting peaking capacity.[5] The AID mission was interested in investigating the possibility of a loan for approximately $18 million, but "felt that seven years was too long a period in which to stretch out loan disbursements."[6] The mission therefore explored the alternative of financing the installation of only two of the four units, amounting to 125 megawatts. It was decided, however, that this alternative "might reduce the attraction of AID financing of the project since the installation of 125 megawatts would require only two turbine-generating machines."[7] In short, the foreign exchange component of a 125-megawatt project would be too low (about $10 million), and the optimal length of time for phasing in 250 megawatts of power capacity would be too long.[8]

In an attempt to make the project more eligible for financing, the mission "asked the company about the possibility of constructing both stages within the five-year period, anticipating Unit No. 3 by one year, and Unit No. 4 by two years."[9] (This issue is discussed in the following section.) Moreover, the mission's list of financed equipment to be imported for a 250-megawatt plant included about $13 million worth of items which could be produced in Brazil.[10] Of this amount, $7 million was to be for imported generators and turbines. It was learned in the course of discussions with the power company, however, that the generator and turbine manufacturers would probably resist, through their manufacturers' association, the attempt to import the equipment.

Although the borrowing company did not mind buying both types of equipment in Brazil, it knew that this would mean $7 million less of a highly-prized type of financing for its project. It would have to make a separate effort to raise those funds on the local market. This would be a difficult task, of course, given the fact that neither a private nor public capital market existed for raising such funds, as in most developing countries. Like many state-sponsored enterprises, moreover, the company had had difficulty in generating its own capital funds because of the political difficulties of obtaining rate increases. Finally, it had already exhausted official domestic loan possibilities when it obtained a $55 million local-cost-equivalent loan from the official development bank. It must have been clear to the company, then, that it had a much better chance of getting the project undertaken in the first place if it were to install the 250 megawatts all at once, and if it were to import as many of the turbines and generators as possible.

On the turbine-generator question, the following sequence of events occurred. In a few previous similar cases in which the Brazilian capital goods industry might have been able to supply a significant amount of a financed project's equipment requirements, the mission had suggested that the borrower pursue a "fifty-fifty" bargaining approach with the industrial association representing their capital goods industry (ABDIB), with respect to any equipment on the import list which could be produced locally.[11] In this case, the mis-

sion suggested to the power company that because locally manufactured turbines had a higher import content (roughly 50 percent) than
did the generators, an agreement be sought with ABDIB to buy the
generators in Brazil and the turbines abroad. (The 250-megawatt
project required two generators and two turbines.)

Although the company had originally stated that it was not averse
to buying all the equipment in Brazil, it accepted the AID suggestion,
since it knew that the probability of obtaining a greater amount of
financing would thereby be considerably increased. When broaching
the subject to ABDIB, however, the company found that the turbine
manufacturers were not willing to accept an arrangement in which
they lost and the generator manufacturers won. It was then suggested
by the mission that the turbine order and generator order each be
divided equally between Brazil and the United States, in order to
avoid the veto of the local manufacturing group that got nothing. The
borrower company, however, considered this solution difficult to
accept: it would mean separate maintenance, training, and spare parts
for each brand of equipment. Hence the company sought to convince
ABDIB to allow the generators to be purchased in Brazil and the
turbines abroad.[12]

The turbine manufacturers were adamant, however, and so a new
formula was painstakingly devised by them and the power company.
According to the formula, the turbines could be imported, but the
bid-winning North American firms would be required to enter into a
joint venture with a Brazilian firm. The local firm's contribution to
manufacture of the equipment would have to be greater than a certain
percentage, which would be fixed according to the past experience of
Brazilian turbine manufacturers in collaboration with foreign firms.

There was much debate over what the Brazilian percentage should
be. The turbine manufacturers argued for a precise figure, rather than
a range, out of their belief that the senior U.S. partner in such a
venture would concede them only the lowest extremity of any range.
The power company and its engineering consultant firm (also present
at the meetings and the subsidiary of a U.S. engineering consulting
firm) argued for a lower percentage expressed as a floor rather than a
range, fearing that a higher fixed percentage would saddle the U.S.
senior partner with an intolerable degree of inflexibility. Discussion
also ranged over whether the percentage should be expressed in terms
of value or in terms of quantity of component parts. The value approach was mistrusted by both sides as an incentive for the U.S. or

Brazilian firm to inflate its costs in order to win a bigger share of the fixed value percentage. The component-parts solution was considered extremely complex: would an estimate be based on the weight or number of the Brazilian-made parts in past Brazilian turbine production?

Another problem was that Brazilian turbine manufacturers' past relationships had been with European producers — as subsidiaries, affiliates, or licensees — and they were not pleased with the idea of a forced partnership with an unknown U.S. firm. The terms of the collaboration were finally agreed upon, although grudgingly. Several months later, after the loan had been approved and signed, and bidding was opened, considerable delay and trouble occurred because of the requirements concerning Brazilian participation placed on the bidding U.S. firms.

I reserve comment on this example until the end of the section. Suffice it to say at this point that an unfortunate aspect of the bargaining process described is that price does not enter as one of the bargaining variables.[13] Since local costs cannot be financed by foreign aid loans, competitive bidding between the local and foreign producer is not possible. Unlike the competitive bidding which the bargaining process replaces, price has no relevance; the buyer (the borrower) and the supplier (local industry) are concerned not with the cost of what they are buying and selling but rather with dividing up the market in a way that will win them the foreign financing. Of course, the borrower will conduct separate competitive biddings for its local and foreign purchases subsequent to the bargaining process. But price considerations have still not been allowed to impinge upon the foreign-domestic purchase decision.

Even though local industry has been brought to a bargaining table in these cases, it has not been encouraged or forced to use price as a bargaining tool. This is an important missed opportunity in a developing country where local industry is often characterized by oligopolistic high-cost patterns that frequently originate in, and are perpetuated by, protective tariff policy. Donor entities themselves often criticize the high-cost structure of local industry as development-stifling, and they exert pressure on borrower-country governments to make policy changes which allow the "fresh winds of competition" to sweep the local manufacturing scene.

Local industry does not resort to price as one of the instruments for bargaining its way through this particular situation probably because of the unusual form that such price competition would take. That is, all parties involved know roughly what amount of foreign exchange would have to be consumed by the project in order to make it worthwhile for a foreign loan. Thus if one local producer of a certain item *did* get a part of the local share of the pie by offering to reduce his price relative to foreign price, then some other local producer would lose his place in the fixed local share.

In other words, the price cutter's gain is not made at the expense of the foreign producer of the same good, who is absent, unknown to the local producer, and not expected to exercise powers of oligopolistic retaliation. Rather, the loser turns out to be the highest-cost (relative to foreign price) local producer of *another* item to be bargained upon. He is a member of the price cutter's own association, and his product (the loser's) is likely to be noncompeting or even complementary — as in the case of the turbines and generators. This may explain why the bargaining process described has not evolved on its own into a colluding variation of competitive bidding. For the price cutter hurts a fellow producer, even though the latter's noncompeting good lies outside the normal concern of an oligopolist's market-dividing pursuits. This particular bargaining process, then, spreads the pall of oligopolistic pricing beyond its usual domain — or, at least, blocks an incentive for local industry to cut its prices.

Given a financing procedure that results in such an *ad hoc* bargaining group, and given the often oligopolistic nature of the local industry involved, it is unfortunate that once the donor organizations violated the market mechanism, they could not go one step further. They might have used this cumbersome vehicle of market-dividing to introduce price incentives as criteria for determining which local industries would compose the local share of the pie: the lenders could have agreed to strike from the import list those items of lowest price relative to foreign price. They might have thereby reconstituted the workings of competition in a rather bizarre way, perhaps even more effective than traditional competitive bidding where circumvention is easily achieved by oligopolistic bidders. Instead, the opposite occurred: the structure of foreign lending *encouraged* local collusion on the projects it financed by providing reasons and occasions for local producers — many of them antagonistic to each other — to come together and learn how to divide up a market amicably.

The Size of the Power Plant

I draw heavily for examples on the power project in southern Brazil, not because it is unique, but because it so succinctly illustrates a general phenomenon I observed at one stage or another in various donor-financed projects. I refer to another project later on, so as not to place the burden of the argument so completely on one particular case.

It was mentioned in the last section that the AID mission suggested that the power company explore the desirability of installing all 250 megawatts within a time period shorter than that originally planned; at the same time, the company was discouraged from seeking a loan for only 125 megawatts of installed capacity. After some mutual reviewing of demand forecasts and construction schedules for other projects in the system, it was decided that the full 250-megawatt installation could be justified. The company said that the original construction schedule

was based solely on demand considerations, *rather than on what was most financially desirable.* After further consideration, the company expressed preference for this suggested compression of the construction schedule: they felt it was less costly financially to have the construction firm working on installation of all four units at once, rather than having to reconvoke the construction team in 1973, after having disbanded it in 1972. With respect to the fact that the last two units installed in 1972 would mean short-term excess capacity, the company said that this excess could be considered as reserve capacity, a 'luxury' it had never had. The company suggested that it would include the last two units in the electricity rate as soon as they were installed, *even if demand did not yet require them.* There would be no cost to the company, therefore, of compressing the construction schedule.[14]

In the meantime, the Brazilian government had commissioned a power forecast and supply study for the three states comprising the southern region; the project was financed by a grant from the UNDP, administered by the IBRD, and carried out by a consortium of Canadian and U.S. engineering firms (CANAMBRA) working with Brazilian counterparts in the government power sector. The study of the southern region followed upon the heels of an earlier pioneer power study of the center-south region, where most of the country's demand for power was concentrated. The two studies represented a concerted effort by the Brazilian government, with the urging and assistance of the donors, to introduce integrated long-range planning into the power sector. Just as important, the power studies were expected to generate some excellent projects for foreign financing, since they would result from a planning experience guided and approved by one of the financing entities, the IBRD. It was hoped, finally, that this experience would help the Brazilian power sector to become self-sustaining in planning for the future needs of its power system.

During the period when the mission and the power company were examining the 125-megawatt question, it became known that the CANAMBRA report would recommend the immediate installation of only 125 megawatts at Passo Real — rather than the 250 megawatts favored by AID. CANAMBRA would further recommend that when peaking capacity became necessary, it would be most economically installed not at Passo Real but at Passo Fundo, another site that had been worked on sporadically in previous years. Upon learning of the impending CANAMBRA recommendation, the mission and the power company requested that CANAMBRA and the Ministry of Mines and Energy consider changing their recommendation to the following: (1) install the peaking capacity at Passo Real instead of Passo Fundo, and (2) explore the feasibility of including the additional 125 megawatts of peaking capacity along with the original installation of 125 megawatts at Passo Real.

The justification accompanying this request was that (1) financing would be available in one lump sum for all 250 megawatts at Passo Real; (2) the installation of 125 megawatts of peaking capacity at Passo Fundo at some future date would entail the undertaking of a totally separate capital project that would be much more costly than the incremental investment required to add two more sets of generators and turbines to the already existing installation at Passo Real; and (3) the inevitable delays that were bound to accompany the loan application procedure and subsequent construction would most likely bring the Passo Real project into service at about the same time for which the need for peaking capacity was projected.

The requested change was responded to affirmatively by CANAMBRA and the ministry after a three- or four-month delay, during which intense discussion and dissension took place among the government power engineers and economists asked to analyze the request. Some felt that the change was not justified by the demand forecast, that the second 125 megawatts of capacity would therefore be installed before it was needed, and that they were being pressured by the ministry to provide a "spurious" technical justification for the change in order to obtain foreign assistance that would be a political feather in the ministry's cap. Others felt that the difference between the efficiency of the two alternatives was not great enough to override the consideration that financing would be available in one lump sum for one alternative and not for the other.

In justifying the change, the AID loan paper recommended that the loan agreement require AID approval of any future decision by the company to undertake construction at Passo Fundo. The requirement was desired because Passo Fundo, like Passo Real, was a favored project in state politics, and it was likely that the state-sponsored power company would be subject to political pressures to undertake it. Moreover, the company had a long history of subjugation to public works politics. It was in a weak financial position because of its overextension in construction of doubtful projects and because it had not been allowed by the state government to charge a rate high enough to cover its costs. The AID loan for 250 megawatts at Passo Real was eventually approved and signed. Shortly thereafter, the company decided to apply for a loan for Passo Fundo, which it obtained two years later from the Inter-American Development Bank.

Suppose the story of the decision to install 250 megawatts at Passo Real had come to the attention of outside observers — Budget Bureau economists, Congressmen, Peterson or Rockefeller report-writers, students of development assistance, muckraking journalists, sympathetic development technicians, critical Latin Americans. It could have been looked upon as totally reasonable, because of the accompanying demand and engineering justifications; or it could have been cited as an example of inefficiency, incompetence, or dishonesty on the part of the parties involved. This is exactly the type of criticism that has been leveled at development assistance programs, with the accompanying recommendation that the quality of personnel be improved, better techniques of analysis be developed, and the program be better protected from the pressures of U.S. manufacturing groups interested in selling products abroad (e.g., doubling the size of Passo Real almost doubled the amount of U.S. equipment imported).

From an organizational point of view, however, all parties involved were not only acting quite efficiently, but they were even pursuing the stated goals of the institutions to which they belonged: they had selected an alternative that could be justified technically, and their solution favored the cause of development — given the constraints imposed upon them.[15] From AID's point of view, the larger project had more chance of being shepherded through the agency and approved. It represented a more efficient use of the agency's administrative capacity, since only import costs could be financed and since the loan application procedure and subsequent project monitoring was elaborate and time-consuming. For the power company, the doubling of the size of the project and the premature installation of the third and fourth units was a small cost to pay for the corresponding increase in the probability of obtaining financing for the first 125 megawatts and for the second two units which would have to be installed sooner or later. For the Brazilian government — trying to ration its scarce domestic resources among competing investment demands in a rapidly growing public sector — any form of financing for Passo Real would be welcomed, since it would eliminate one source of demand for public investment funds.

The costs to the economy of this type of decision are obvious: (1) in a capital-scarce country, a lump-sum investment was being made when the demand forecasts and the technology of the project offered the opportunity for staggered development — an opportunity seldom encountered in capital projects, whose technological indivisibility frequently results in costly excess capacity for some time; (2) a state company trying to shake off a history of financial problems and overextension in doubtful projects was encouraged to undertake a project larger than it had originally desired; (3) finally, on the grounds of expediency, there was tampering with a pioneering attempt to introduce long-range integrated planning into the power sector — the type of planning that was considered vital to the protection of electric power investments from political pressures to build unsound projects. The tampering, needless to say, reduced the credibility of the planning attempt in the eyes of those Brazilians engaged in it. It reduced the credibility of the development entities who, despite their promotion and financing of the planning effort, were the first to subject it to the pressures it was meant to resist.

One important question has been glossed over: Which decision was best from a strictly technical point of view — the 125 megawatts or the 250 megawatts, the turbines manufactured in Brazil or those made abroad? As can be gathered from the story, a respectable technical defense could be made for *both* decisions in both cases, without recourse to arguments concerning private and social costs. In the turbine case, any problem of local inexperience could have been dealt with, as is normally done, by requiring performance bonds and/or technical supervision by the foreign licensing firm. The power company's change of heart about its willingness to buy the turbines in Brazil, and about the necessity for 250 megawatts instead of 125, represented a moving-about among technically respectable alternatives, goaded by the incentives and disincentives of foreign assistance procedures. In this instance, the goad was the decrease in the "price" of using imported equipment, triggered by the knowledge that the amount of the loan and the probability of obtaining it would be greater if more equipment were imported.

The one and only technical choice rarely exists. This is particularly apparent in developing countries, where knowledge about how things work is incipient, and where uncertainties are greater about the future and about resource availabilities, costs, and returns. Even though few technicians would argue this point, technical choices are nevertheless frequently defended as if they were the one and only solution; correspondingly, project analysis technique is looked upon as the path leading to that unique solution. The more that institutions must justify their choices publicly, the more obscured are the underlying factors that tip the scales in one direction or another, and the more prevalent is the impression that there is such an absolute as the "true" technical choice. Contributing to this impression is the emphasis placed by donors on cost-benefit analyses and engineering feasibility studies as requirements for proving the technical legitimacy of the project selected.

The striving for technical excellence emphasized in the recommendations of official reports on development assistance implies that the more sophisticated the engineer and the economist, and the more effort that is devoted to devising sharp instruments of analysis, the closer one will come to the single technically correct answer — like Michelangelo's statement that the art of sculpture consists of chiseling away at an amorphous block of marble until one "discovers" the perfect form embedded in it. Also implicit in the recommendations for better-designed cost-benefit analyses and more sophisticated economists is the belief that the resulting choices will come to approximate the rationality that would have been spontaneously generated by the workings of a Smithian hand in a perfectly competitive market.

But as the last two examples show, there are no rock-bottom truths waiting to be uncovered by project analysis techniques. Buying the turbines or even the generators abroad was technically justifiable, just as was their purchase at home. To buy the equipment abroad, however, involved a lost opportunity to assist the local manufacturing sector in doing what it had not done before. Local purchase would have made it possible for local industry, the next time around, to build a 76-horsepower Francis turbine by itself. Likewise, the decisions to install 250 megawatts instead of 125, and to execute the project in five years instead of seven, were as technically justifiable as their opposites. But the 250-megawatt, five-year decision meant a greater cost, economically and institutionally. It involved a meddling by assistance entities in recipient-country decisionmaking and increased skepticism about the use of analytical techniques in project selection. The policies and organizational structure of development assistance, however, had determined that the "true" technical decision lay in importing the equipment and building the plant larger and faster.

Highway Maintenance Equipment, and the Earth vs. Rockfill Dam

Another brief example concerns the designing of a $31.5 million highway maintenance equipment loan for the three southern states of Brazil. The equipment list drawn up by AID mission engineers was based on an equipment-per-mile ratio *higher* than that in the United States.[16] From a technical point of view, the justification was sound: (1) the roads to be maintained were in such poor condition that a major catching up would be necessary before routine U.S.-type maintenance could be carried out; (2) rainfall was heavier than in the United States; (3) traffic on earth and gravel roads was much heavier than U.S. traffic; (4) legal axle loads exceeded those in the United States, thus requiring heavier maintenance; and (5) Brazilian maintenance personnel were less skilled than their U.S. counterparts. Moreover, the program was based on the goal of "optimum maintenance" for a large percentage of the roads — i.e., maintenance of the road at its original design standards and performance. By the time the roads were in a condition good enough for simple routine maintenance, it was said, much of the equipment would be spent and replacement could be scaled down to a level consistent with routine maintenance.

Needless to say, the technical logic of the solution excluded other important considerations. For example, was "optimum maintenance" a desirable goal in a country with much less capital than the United States, where this standard was formulated? Also, would faltering maintenance divisions in highway departments with a penchant for construction be able to absorb such a massive dose of new equipment and such a spurt in the intensity of their maintenance? Or would some of the abundant equipment be siphoned off into highway construction, as had happened in other maintenance loans, thus reinforcing the vicious circle of construction-without-maintenance?

There was no reason for the AID engineers or their counterparts in the Brazilian state highway departments to be encouraged or forced to include these considerations in their reasoning. As far as their organizational context was concerned, the more equipment the better. For the borrower entity the larger the equipment list, the better the chances for getting financing. For the lender entity, the chances for "producing" a given amount of capital transfer would be greater with a larger equipment list. As usual, the positive correlation between the size of a loan and the possibility of obtaining or making it was related to the imported equipment list through the policy of financing mainly foreign exchange costs: maintenance was more equipment-intensive than construction, which requires much more local expenditure on materials and labor; and equipment was an importable item, especially if it were sophisticated, and hence unlikely to be produced locally.

One clearly sees the large-project large-import bias in the file memoranda that chronicle the evolution of this loan. Early in the negotiations between the borrower states and the local construction equipment manufacturers' association (GEIMEC), it was argued by GEIMEC that the original import list should be reduced from $35.5 million to $11.7 million to eliminate imported items that could be produced by local industry. The AID mission felt, however, that "this would place too great a burden on the [three] states to finance their share of the program which already includes the purchase of other Brazilian manufactured equipment."[17] A transfer of items from the import to the local-purchase list, in short, would mean less AID financing to the borrower.[18]

In a draft letter to GEIMEC, AID argued that "the currently proposed equipment purchase program as modified by GEIMEC's recommendations would seriously strain the highway budgets of the three states. . . . it may be necessary for the states to negotiate with the Sindicato [GEIMEC] and national industry on a reasonable division of procurement between imports and national production which recognizes the limited financial resources of the states."[19] AID's "basic strategy" on the equipment objected to by GEIMEC was "to remain firm on large items and bend on smaller ones if necessary, so as not to place an undue burden on financial capacities of states."[20] It was in the interest of AID and the southern states, in sum, to get as much equipment in the loan, and as much locally produced equipment on the import list, as possible. This interest was not a matter of policy but of the necessity to "produce" as organizations.

The last brief example is taken, again, from the Passo Real hydro-electric project. During the time that AID and the power company were working on the loan application, an engineering design firm contracted by the power company was studying the feasibility of a rockfill dam as opposed to an earth dam. It looked as though the difference between the two alternatives would turn out to be marginal in terms of cost, and that in engineering terms, either choice would be feasible. AID was aware that the decision had not yet been made, and it had also been informed that a rockfill dam would require a consid-erably larger amount, and a different type, of heavy construction machinery than the earth dam. It was known, moreover, that local construction firms did not have an equipment fleet large enough for, or suited to, that particular task. If the rockfill alternative were selected, then, it would be necessary for the local contractors to acquire about $5.5 million of heavy construction machinery, most of it not made in Brazil.

If the extra expenditure for construction equipment could be in-cluded as part of the financing, from AID's point of view, the power project loan would be larger and therefore more desirable. Arrange-ments could be made whereby the power company would buy the equipment and lease or sell it to the contractors; the lease or sale price, of course, would have to reflect the lower depreciation and interest costs permitted by the favorable terms of the AID loan (6 percent, five years grace, 25 years amortization). At this juncture, AID advised the engineering firm of the possibility of including the construction equipment in the loan, if the decision were for a rockfill dam. The firm, in turn, incorporated this consideration into the cost calcula-tions for the two alternatives: the equipment input into the rockfill alternative was priced in accordance with the favorable terms of the AID loan, while the cost of the earth dam was calculated at the prices normally charged by local contractors for their individually pur-chased equipment — prices which embodied much higher deprecia-tion and interest costs than those allowed by the terms of the AID loan. When the design firm completed its feasibility study, the rockfill alternative was chosen as the most economic. AID increased its pro-jected loan to the power company by $5.5 million for purchase of construction machinery in the United States.

The rockfill dam decision was technically flawless. Moreover, the favoring by all parties involved of a capital and foreign-exchange-intensive construction technique was perfectly rational, for the additional foreign exchange component associated with this technique increased considerably the possibility of obtaining financing for the project. The only factor that was missing from these considerations was a sense of the country's capital and foreign exchange scarcity, a consideration which was overridden by the way foreign exchange was perceived in this organizational world and by the primacy of the question as to whether the project would be financed at all.

Conclusion

The complex detail of my examples is the only way to convey how the foreign exchange financing of projects, combined with the organizational desirability of large projects, affects economic decisionmaking. Just as important, the details reveal that this imposition of private and social costs on the economy of the aided country is not inflicted unilaterally by the donor entity, but is *collaborated upon by the damaged parties* — the borrower, the local government (when it is distinct from the borrower), and the local producer. In the case of the turbines, for example, the borrower originally told mission technicians that it would just as soon buy the equipment at home. By the end of the negotiations, when it became clear that local purchase would jeopardize the loan itself or decrease its size, the borrower was then arguing that the specifications required for this particular turbine could not be met by Brazilian industry or could not be met on time.

Local industry's "collaboration" in such cases is influenced by the fact that it is likely to benefit from the undertaking of a public works project because of the considerable local expenditure generated by such projects — regardless of how many orders are lost to imports. Hence the manufacturers' association is willing to give in on some items, allowing them to be imported and thus seeming to act against the very interests it was formed to protect. To local industry, just as in the case of the borrower, the decision about whether individual orders for equipment are to be placed at home or abroad is secondary to the basic question of whether or not the project will be undertaken at all. In developing countries, that question is frequently determined by whether or not foreign financing is obtained.

The above examples show that considerable resentment was gen-

erated between local manufacturing groups and the donor organization by the haggling that took place between the borrower and these
groups, often over sums that were insignificant in relation to the total
amount of the loan (e.g., the cumbersome bargain struck over the
turbines would add $1.5 million to a $23 million loan). During the
meeting at which the final turbine arrangement was hammered out,
the local manufacturers grumbled throughout about how development assistance biddings — whether AID, IBRD, or IDB — were
always "fixed" to make developed-country manufacturers win out.
Various past projects were mentioned in evidence. On the one hand,
then, local manufacturers express virulent criticism of development
assistance to their colleagues and countrymen, characterizing it as an
unfair hypocritical program serving donor-country business. On the
other hand, however, the hurt groups publicly deny being hurt, or
will not support public allegations to that effect, because they will
always benefit to some extent from any public works project. Hence
the donor organization is severely and publicly criticized by beneficiary groups and at the same time is not able to enlist these critics as
allies in its internal attempts to change the criticized procedures.[21]

One question remains. Are the stories and lessons of this chapter
unique to Brazil or to AID? Certainly, in a smaller or less-developed
country there would not have been local manufacturers to contend so
bitterly for the electric power project described in this chapter. The
manufacturing sector of such countries is not likely to be significant
enough to require any decision about whether to import. The stories
told in this chapter, however, illustrate a decisionmaking process that
does not require a well-developed local industry in order to go wrong.
Projects can still be too big, domestic sources of supply neglected, and
relative factor scarcities disrespected, without the existence of a
domestic manufacturing industry. In fact, the somewhat atypical
existence of a large equipment-manufacturing sector in Brazil may
have made it possible to get a glimpse of the problematical decisionmaking in the first place. In a country less developed than Brazil, the
neglected domestic supplies, the simpler technologies, or the smaller
projects would be quite difficult to find. They would not be embodied
in bypassed persons, groups, or industries, and they would not have
the ardent spokesmen that a developed manufacturing sector has. The
Brazilian setting, then, was perhaps one of the few where the process
of neglecting better alternatives could be so clearly observed.[22]

Chapter Six

FINANCING IMPORTS

The obvious cause of some of the problems outlined above is that development assistance entities tend to limit their financing to the foreign exchange components of projects. The U.S. aid program is required by procedure to limit most of its project financing to import costs, although presidential directives in the fall of 1965 allowed for local-cost financing in agriculture, education, health, and, more recently, population planning and nutrition. Despite this relaxation, more than 80 pecent of total AID funds continue to be spent in the United States.[1] The import-cost constraint is not peculiar to bilateral assistance. The IBRD's Articles of Agreement limit financing to the foreign exchange cost of projects, though with some exceptions; foreign exchange costs account for about 75 percent of its financing. The IDB can be somewhat more liberal about local currency financing, since it can draw on the local-currency contributions of its member-borrowers; nevertheless, only about 25 percent of its financing goes toward local costs.[2]

The policy of financing only import costs is a separate issue from that of tying aid to donor-country exports, with which I am not concerned here. Even though the United States has "untied" its aid to the extent that it allows procurement of aid-financed goods in some third countries, these funds still finance only import costs.[3] The IBRD and the IDB allow for some bidding by local suppliers on certain items and are prepared to finance the items if the recipient-country bidder wins. Though these organizations have in recent years allowed a 15 to 25 percent price advantage to the recipient-country bidder, this action has not resulted in significant aid-financed purchases from recipient-country industry. Though I refer in what follows to the "policy of financing only import costs," then, it should be understood that some local-cost financing is allowed by all donor organizations, and that the U.S. program has become less restrictive in this area. As the data show, however, the major part of development assistance financing goes for import costs.

The tendency to shy away from financing the local-cost portions of a project has a long history originating in the financing made available to eastern European governments during the interwar period.[4] In general, development assistance designers tend to think that the local costs of financed projects are better taken care of by the recipient country. Local-cost expenditure is considered to be less easily monitored and more subject to possible diversion to wasteful use than foreign exchange costs. Foreign exchange, moreover, is considered a scarcity less easily remedied than a shortage of domestic savings; the latter, it is felt, can be dealt with by the recipient country through improvement of tax-collecting administration and changes in fiscal policy. Such steps will prove, according to this rationale, that the borrower country is genuinely committed to the development plans for which it is seeking assistance.[5] Finally, local-cost financing is considered problematic to the extent that it may carry with it potentially inflationary effects.

Whether or not these justifications are valid (see pages 79-83), the result is that the availability of project financing for only foreign exchange costs causes the priorities of recipient countries to almost invisibly rearrange themselves around foreign-exchange-intensive projects and encourages maximization of the foreign exchange component of any desired project. Thus although development financing at concessional terms is supposed to help recipient countries overcome their foreign exchange scarcity, the form of the financing nevertheless creates an incentive to increase unnecessarily the demand for that scarce exchange. Such demand is increased beyond what it would be if the financing for projects were offered, for example, on a percentage-of-the-total-cost basis, regardless of the distribution between local and foreign exchange; or if financing were provided as general budgetary support for a previously determined mix of public sector investments. As the last chapter's examples show, the availability of development assistance for the financing of only the foreign exchange costs of projects has just as significant an effect on the decisionmaking of the donor institution as it has on the countries seeking financing. This chapter focuses on the effect on the borrower and the following chapter on the donor.

Before proceeding, I briefly summarize the flaws in a process whereby aid-recipient countries economize on the use of domestic savings relative to aid-provided foreign exchange. The process undermines the planning and execution of economic development priorities in both the borrowing country and lending institution by introducing a constraint which seriously conflicts with certain development goals. The very logic of development lending is to encourage economic rationality in decisionmaking and to discourage "irresponsibility" and its syndrome of extravagant capital projects. But development assistance incentives make the extravagant project the most rational choice for a developing country to make. The incentives cause the smaller project to be left out, even though it may have a better chance of being absorbed by the economy.

If a country is arranging its public sector budget in order to maximize the amount of foreign-exchange-using projects and the amount of foreign exchange spent on any particular project, then it is not giving adequate emphasis to the task of channeling as much investment demand as is feasible into the local economy. One of the major development benefits of a public sector investment program — the generation of demand for local production — is thus forfeited. A public investment program generates a type of demand for intermediate goods and capital that is unique; its long term and large scale cause certain production possibilities to cross the threshold of financial feasibility. The piecemeal and short-term nature of private sector demand, in contrast, can leave untouched many of the production possibilities still to be activated in a developing country.

Another problem caused by the availability of foreign financing solely for foreign exchange costs is the resulting increase in the borrower country's current and future foreign exchange requirements; this, in turn, exacerbates the stifling character of the foreign exchange bottleneck on the country's attempts to progress. The problem does not result from the fact that foreign exchange financing is supplied in the first place; rather, the availability of the financing exclusively for foreign exchange costs (1) leads to an increase in the foreign exchange component of a proposed project that normally would not have occurred, (2) increases the proportion of foreign exchange intensive projects in the government's public sector investment program, and (3) increases future demand for foreign exchange because of the need for spare parts and replacement equipment to service the financed project. The last is particularly costly, since these expenditures normally do not qualify for development assistance.

The structure of development lending, then, increases unnecessarily the burden on the borrower's future payments balances and encourages the type of irrational decisionmaking said to be characteristic of underdevelopment. At the same time that development assistance incentives are attracting large projects, assistance advisers are trying to stamp out monetary and fiscal irresponsibility and encourage a foreign exchange policy that will bring the borrower country's import demands within the bounds of its export earnings. Given the difficulties and serious costs to a developing-country government of faithfully pursuing such a stabilization policy, these unnecessary additions to foreign exchange needs are certainly undesirable.

Another counterproductive effect of the project lending structure has to do with a set of attitudes also considered part of the underdevelopment syndrome. Addiction to the foreign-made product is common among developing-country elites. Even when the local product reaches or surpasses the quality of the imported one, the consumer often continues to prefer the import. The economic histories of developing countries often characterize depressions, wars, and other drastic import-blocking catastrophies as blessings in disguise: while disruptive, they forced the adamant consumer to try the local product and get used to it. Although the discussion of developing-country preferences for imports usually centers on luxury and other consumer goods, these import preferences are often just as prevalent in the capital and intermediate-goods sector.

To the extent that the preference of the intermediate-goods consumer for the imported good prevails, the repercussions of an investment project will be forgone by the local economy. The development assistance project thus bears some analogy to the underdeveloped-country railway that leads directly from a foreign-owned mining site to the coast, instead of traversing the country and picking up inputs and dropping off outputs along the way. Both aid project and railway have only minor repercussions on the economy.

Local industry's ties to foreign suppliers, combined with resistance to local procurement even when cost and quality are favorable, pose one of the important institutional obstacles to self-sustaining growth. Development assistance adds to the problem by making it easier and more efficient to look for designs and products abroad rather than at home. Thus, the self-help rationale for not financing local-currency costs may in reality turn out to have a "self-hurt" effect.[6] I am not proposing that local products be favored indiscriminately but rather that development assistance not be made available at the cost of neglecting existing possibilities for resource use, for public saving, and for the devising of solutions that work well in the recipient country.

In that the policy of financing only foreign exchange costs leads to import-intensive projects, it induces capital-intensive choices as well. Embodied in imported equipment is the relative labor scarcity of the developed world from which it came. Thus, even if one decreed that development assistance would finance only labor-using technologies and project mixes, it would be difficult to find them, tried and proven, in the donor world. Indeed, the literature of development assistance came to the conclusion some years ago that there was no pool of labor-using and efficient technologies, and that the developing world was stuck with the capital-intensity of the industrial countries. According to this conclusion, the capital-intensity of aided projects was the result of the state of the technological arts, and not of the policy of financing only imports.

More recently, however, studies of specific industries or technology decisions have started to appear, showing that many labor-using technologies are in use and working efficiently in developing countries.[7] These working technologies were in existence, but were passed over, when decisions were made to adopt the more capital-intensive choice for the foreign-financed project.[8] Of course the newly discovered old technologies would not have involved the amount of importing required by the developed-world technologies. The decision to subsidize imports rather than total project costs, then, was an inadvertent decision to favor capital-using choices. The labor-using alternatives were not passed over purposely. They simply were not relevant to the decisions of donor and recipient about how to put together a financeable project or program.

Much of the literature of economic development has evolved in response to intense interest by development assistance organizations and an almost desperate search on their part for the right ways to go about economic development. The imprint of this consumer demand for knowledge is very noticeable in the subject matter and policy orientation of the literature in this field. The policy of financing only imports, then, may have contributed to the lateness of the literature in stumbling upon labor-using technologies that were working well. It was not that such research was discouraged; rather, there was no urgent demand for this type of finding. More recently, in contrast, employment-creating strategies have taken on central importance in development assistance strategies and, as a result, an abundance of literature on the matter has appeared. In that this new concern is not explicitly related to the local-cost financing question, however, it has had little impact on it. (The reasons are discussed in the conclusion to chapter 7.)

The influence of the policy of financing only imports exerts itself not only in the choice of technology for a particular project. More important, it leaves out of the running for financing certain types of activities that are usually more labor-using or complementary to labor use: operational costs as opposed to investment, and decentralized programs as opposed to centralized ones. Take highways, for example. Highway construction was for a long time one of the favored recipients of development assistance, although in recent years the donor world has made a determined effort to reduce that favor. Developing-country roads are famous for their poor maintenance. For this reason, the highway construction loan documents of aid organizations usually paid standard obeisance to "the maintenance problem," and required "that the borrower maintain its road system adequately."[9] To this end, imported maintenance equipment and consulting services were sometimes included in the construction loan. But even when maintenance was financed as a separate project, most of the expenditure went toward imported highway maintenance equipment and consulting services and was based on developed-world combinations of machines and men — as in the AID-type loan discussed on pages 68-70. The ongoing operating expenditures for maintenance, mainly labor and fuel, would customarily fall outside the scope of the financed items. Maintenance would also lose out in the allocation of scarce budgetary resources in the recipient country, precisely because of its "dependence on current budget expenditure for which foreign financing is generally not available, and its relative lack of glamor compared with new construction."[10]

The fact that adequate current budgetary resources usually got diverted from maintenance was the principal cause of the maintenance problem in the first place. The donor world's response to the problem, however, was not to finance the activity itself; rather, it tried to gain assurances from the borrower "that adequate current budgetary resources [would be] devoted to this purpose." The problem, then, could never be adequately dealt with by import-financed construction or maintenance loans, for the financing procedure excluded both expenditures that were directly labor-using and expenditures for items like fuel that were complementary to labor use. Operating and local expenditures, in short, were outside the reach of a program accustomed to financing imports.

The financing of operations and decentralized expenditures is made difficult not only by a policy of financing only import costs. It also runs counter to an organizational economy inherent in large projects, the subject of the following chapter. I interrupt the discussion here, then, until the large-project question is dealt with in the next chapter. In the conclusion, I comment at length on the donor world's recognition of the capital bias problem and the attempt to deal with it.

FOREIGN ASSISTANCE AS A SUBSTITUTE FOR DOMESTIC SAVINGS

Implicit in the rationale for financing only import costs is the assumption that when abundant foreign exchange project financing is dangled before the eyes of a capital-scarce country, the latter will be highly motivated to raise the complementary domestic resources for the project on its own — something it might never have done without the incentive of a foreign exchange loan. Just as important, according to the rationale, the necessity of financing the local-cost portion of a project forces the developing country to improve its fiscal policy, provides it with the experience of carrying out a specific revenue-raising effort, and gives it the knowledge that such an effort can succeed. This try at "self-help" by the borrower is considered a benefit in itself, above and beyond the new public sector services to be supplied by the financed project.

It is important to make clear the fallacy in the rationale, since it is one of the important justifications for the foreign-exchange-only and project approaches to development assistance.[11] The rationale is based on the explicit assumption that aid-supplied foreign exchange is perceived by recipient countries as a *complement* to domestic resources. Yet it is clear from the examples of the last chapter that the availability of development assistance in this form causes borrower countries to perceive such foreign exchange as an *alternative* to the raising of domestic revenues.[12]

A developing-country government seeking an increase in the flow of domestic saving to the public sector will meet with political and administrative difficulties. Even if such efforts are successful, the government must nevertheless pay serious political costs in terms of the public ire that will be provoked by increased taxes or the ill will of prominent businessmen and politicians affected by crackdowns on income tax collections. Achieving a foreign assistance loan, in contrast, is in no way fraught with political difficulties expected to arise in the course of seeking the loan or as a result of obtaining it. On the contrary, the winning of foreign financing represents the stamp of approval by the international credit community, and thus it is of considerable political benefit to a developing-country government. It is likely, then, that the domestic resources mobilized for an aid-financed project may not be truly additional, but are simply diverted from other programs. Such resources may comprise public sector investment mixes which have been rearranged so as to *minimize* the self-help content, with the hope of maximizing the supply of foreign assistance.[13]

The perception by the borrower country of donor foreign exchange as an alternative rather than a complement to domestic resources applies even more to the individual borrower entity. The latter has no responsibility for the monetary and fiscal policy of his country and thus need not be concerned over the repercussions of his investment decisions on that policy. The borrower entity, that is, sees foreign assistance funds as the investment capital it seeks rather than as scarce foreign exchange. The borrower government, in contrast, *is* concerned with the supply of foreign exchange as related to the expected demand for it. This concern will, at the least, place some upper limits on the tendency to rearrange public investment mixes in import-intensive ways.

Strange as it may seem, the borrower entity tends to perceive the supply of foreign assistance as virtually infinite. Despite general knowledge that the total supply of such funds is exceedingly scarce in relation to the needs of the developing world, the individual borrower nevertheless sees the world as if he were an atomistic consumer in a perfectly competitive market: the amount of assistance financing he seeks is an insignificant percentage of total world supply, and any single purchase (a loan) by him or another "consumer" will not, in his eyes, significantly alter that supply or its price. As in any perfectly competitive consumer market, the goods (foreign financing) are his for the asking, as long as he can pay the "price." In his eyes, the price is the putting together of a project proposal which qualifies for such financing. Part of the qualification, of course, is a foreign exchange component large enough to make the project worthy of consideration by the lending institution.

Although rationing criteria may be applied to development assistance by the donor agency on political, sectoral, or regional grounds, this does not change the borrower's perception of such funds as in infinite supply. The applicant, usually well-informed of such rationing criteria, incorporates them into his concept of the qualified project. If the criteria exclude him, he does not seek financing. Hence those borrowers who try for foreign assistance financing are already a self-screened group who think they can "pay the price." If they fail to obtain a loan, they think it is because their project is not adequate rather than because the supply of financing is in any way limited.[14] Part of the reason that the borrower considers the supply of foreign assistance exchange as abundant, in sum, is because he relates it to the size of the single demand he is making.

Contrast this perceived infinite supply of foreign exchange investment capital to the way the borrower looks at the supply of *public* financing in his own country. The public sector borrower in a developing country has no access to the private capital market or to public bond flotations, since such avenues of public finance normally do not exist. Moreover, a major part of the government budget is committed to unavoidable current expenditures, for which the borrower's project capital does not qualify. What remains is the public sector investment budget and the credit of official development banks, if the latter exist. The individual borrower's demands for financing, in short, represent a much larger proportion of the expected supply of domestic financing than of the total supply of foreign assistance funds. Hence his perception of domestic supply as acutely finite.

Contributing to this perception of domestic capital as scarce in relation to foreign assistance capital is the location in the borrower's own land of the source of supply, the allocation process, and the other contenders. The borrower is completely familiar with the way official domestic capital has been allocated in the past, with the various public personages contending for part of that supply, and with the fact that the cumulative demands for financing always turn out to be greater than official funds forthcoming. The borrower knows that a process of elimination will occur, and he is acquainted with the people who do it and how it is done. He knows that his gain of official capital will be at the loss of another contender, with whom he is probably acquainted. He knows that a "qualified" project will not be enough to secure him funds on the domestic capital market and that he will also have to politick vigorously, bargain, make payoffs, and assuage losers. In other words, familiarity with the world in which domestic capital is contended for contributes to the public borrower's perception of an acutely finite supply of domestic capital. Conversely, part of the perceived infinity of the supply of foreign assistance capital has to do with the individual borrower's distance from the world of foreign assistance suppliers and other borrowers — how they proceed, who loses, and what rationing criteria are applied. In the eyes of the single borrower, the vastness of this latter universe makes the supply of capital flowing from it seem infinite.

Individual borrowers, one would think, would still consider the two sources of financing as complements: the easy-to-get (with a qualified project) foreign financing, complemented by the harder-to-get domestic financing. But, because foreign assistance financing discriminates between local and foreign project costs, this is not true. Since such aid limits itself to import expenditures, the borrower sees foreign and domestic credit as *substitutes* for each other, rather than complements, over a wide range of items. One can minimize demand for the scarce good — domestic credit — by moving to the import list some items which could be procured locally, thereby maximizing demand for the "more easily attainable" foreign assistance.[15]

Because the borrower knows that both the minimum project size and foreign exchange component that will provide access to foreign financing are considerably higher than for official domestic credit, he will gladly tailor his project size and composition to these exigencies. The sum total of numerous potential borrowers with this same perception acts as a magnet on the selection of a project's components and on the arrangement of a public sector investment program. It attracts imported items and repels local ones, and it draws toward the center of priority those public sector projects with higher foreign exchange components.

The net self-help result of the availability of foreign exchange project financing, in conclusion, may be that countries shuffle their domestic priorities in favor of the types of local-cost expenditures that are complementary to foreign-exchange-intensive public investment programs.[16] The availability of foreign assistance, in sum, has caused the borrower country to quite rationally switch around its priorities and increase the foreign exchange component of its public sector investment projects in order to get *more* investment out of the *same* amount of domestic revenue.

THE POLICYMAKER AND THE PROJECTMAKER

How can the foregoing discussion be reconciled with the fact that foreign exchange scarcity looms large in the daily preoccupations of the macroeconomic policymakers of the borrower country? Government officials facing foreign exchange shortfalls must not only decide upon the appropriate counteracting policy measures, but must also calculate the political and economic costs that are associated with almost every one of such measures. They are constantly threatened with the cost of pursuing policies that consume too much foreign exchange and, at the same time, they must pay the political costs associated with foreign-exchange-saving measures.

Foreign exchange scarcity is just as much present in the decision-making context of the borrower-country macroeconomic policymaker as it is *absent* in the mind of the project designer or promoter. The costs to the finance minister associated with foreign exchange extravagance and the measures to counteract it do not exist for the projectmaker. Indeed, as indicated above, the using up of foreign exchange by the projectmaker is often associated with *benefits* rather than costs (the increased possibility of outside financing). The two levels of decisionmaking must, of course, be tangent at some point. The finance or planning minister, superior in power and responsibility to the projectmaker, must impose his sense of scarcity on the sum total of government-sponsored expenditures. As pointed out before, however, the numerous decisions that go into this sum total are buried deeply within it; the rejected designs and the rejected projects are usually out of sight. It would be physically impossible for a finance minister to review each bundle of decisions, moreover, rearranging it according to his sense of foreign exchange scarcity. And finally, it is because of this very sense of scarcity that the policymaker considers foreign exchange financing, even if it is embodied in projects, as desirable.

The coexistence in the aid-recipient country of decisionmaking based on two radically different conceptions of foreign exchange scarcity is remarkable. It has probably gone unnoted for several reasons. First, the responsibility of coping with foreign exchange scarcity, in contrast to that of formulating projects, is a function of those higher up in borrower-country and lender institutions. The actions and pronouncements of these functionaries are much more in view than those of the projectmakers. Moreover, policies meant to deal with foreign exchange scarcity have extensive and highly visible repercussions in the financial and political world of a developing country. Government officials frequently explain this foreign exchange problem to the public in their attempts to justify the hardships they are imposing with such policies. An awareness of this scarcity therefore comes to penetrate the public's understanding of development and development assistance problems. The projectmaker's decisions, in contrast, rarely have such visible and extensive effects on the public. When such effects are clearly traceable, as in the case of the local producer who is passed over in favor of a foreign supplier, the injured party's complaint and the official justification for the action tend to take place behind closed doors and at very low levels of the decisionmaking structure, as illustrated by the turbine-generator story of the last chapter.

In other words, an action taken on the grounds of foreign exchange scarcity at the macroeconomic level is perceived by the actiontaker as such, is felt by those affected as such, and is publicly justified as such. At the project level, however, the effect of an individual action based on the perception of relative foreign exchange abundance is not visible at the moment the decision is taken; it has significant effect only in the form of a sum total of many individual decisions. Moreover, the projectmaker is hardly even aware that he has placed a relatively "abundant" valuation on foreign exchange, let alone that this valuation is influencing his decisionmaking. This is in direct contrast to the macroeconomic policymaker, whose job it is to act on his perception of foreign exchange scarcity.[17]

Chapter Seven

THE ORGANIZATIONAL ECONOMY
OF LARGE PROJECTS

The development assistance programmer or macroeconomist is concerned with the supply of aid funds as related to total needs, based on his projections of estimated foreign exchange and savings "gaps" in the developing countries. Or, he may look at the supply of development assistance funds as a function of the developed world's ability to pay — that is, in relation to what those funds could be if donor countries would back their commitment to assistance with a certain percentage of their national income. Either way of looking at the relative supply of these funds gives a prognosis of acute scarcity.[1]

The supply of funds as seen from within the donor organization, in contrast, is perceived in relation not to total estimates of need and supply but to the amount of work or time required to commit the funds available. By job definition, the member of a development assistance organization is charged with finding worthy projects for the funds available. His perception of the supply of these funds is related to the availability of financeable projects. Because long delays and considerable work accompany the putting together of project proposals, there may be fewer financeable projects, at any given moment in time, than funds available. From the employee's point of view, the scarce commodity is frequently the project rather than the funds.

The bureaucrat's perception of foreign exchange supply in a development assistance organization encompasses not only resource quantities but also the *process* in time by which the resources are transferred. By considering organizational tasks and procedures along with total funds, one opens the door to a discussion of both the organizational world of development assistance, and the standards of career performance by which the individual guides his actions and is judged by his superiors. This chapter, then, is distinct from the previous discussion of the effects of a particular policy. I want to show here how the workings of independent bureaucratic phenomena merge with and reinforce the effects of that policy.

It is generally recognized that the transfer of a given amount of development assistance takes a long time under the various methods of transfer that have been tried until now. This happens because of administrative complexities on both sides; because developing country governments may not be institutionally equipped to produce the kind of bureaucratic output required to qualify for and later monitor such assistance; and because the borrower does not have the professional resources to provide the kind of project analysis (engineering, economic, financial) that could go into a hopper out of which donor organizations would make selections. All these factors make up what is generally referred to as "absorptive capacity" of the borrrower country, although it is clear that the *modus operandi* of the donor institution itself contributes to the limitations on resource absorption.

Less obvious than the "low absorptive capacity" of aid-recipient countries is the effect that the slowness of resource transfer has on the nature of the lending institution. Much of the initiative and work involved in generating public projects in developing countries has been transferred gradually from its usual location — a country's public sector institutions — to the lending institution. On the one hand, this is an inadvertent result of the donor organization's attempts to lessen delay in the rate of resource transfer. On the other, it also represents an explicit recognition by the lending institution that the borrower's difficulty in generating "aidworthy" projects is part of the very underdevelopment that foreign assistance is supposed to help change. Much of the development agency's effort, then, is devoted to working out project design with the borrower. For the same reason, much of the agency's staff time is spent drumming up future business — exploring possibilities for projects with borrower governments, suggesting ways of preparing project applications, or making its own evaluation of sectors in which conditions for lending are favorable (e.g., adequate rates in electric power) and then looking closely at those sectors for possible projects. Indeed, the IBRD originally hoped to stay away from such project generation activities, but found, eventually, that it could not:

The initial position of the Bank was that preparation of a project was the responsibility of the borrower; if the Bank became involved, it could not thereafter be sufficiently objective in appraising the project. Though buttressed by logic, this position soon gave way to the pressure of events. "Experience has demonstrated that we do not get enough good projects to appraise unless we are involved intimately in their identification and preparation."[2]

Project identification and preparation amounts to a generation of demand for aid funds. Because lending institutions must pay so much attention to project creation, the nature of these institutions turns out to be quite different from what one would expect. One would imagine the task of an aid institution to be the channeling of a flow of capital or appropriate revenues toward the most worthy of competitive claimants — "worthiness" being defined by criteria such as need, economic efficiency, financial feasibility, political considerations, and sectoral priorities. When funds are seen in this way, then the major preoccupation of the adminstrator is to ration the flow; the major constraint upon his work is the scarcity of funds, and his decisions will be influenced by that sense of scarcity. The activities, concerns, and discussions taking place within the donor organization, one would think, would revolve around decisions relating to the best criteria for rationing funds and to which of the many claimants were most qualified.

As seen above, however, the money does not really flow. "Consumer demand" is not exerted with typical strength because of the institutional factors cited above. Hence the supplier of funds, the assistance institution, has to take over part of the activities typically carried out by the interested consumer: before the supplier can "sell" his funds, he must first help to generate demand for them.[3] When resources are seen in this way — as an inert mass which will not move without great effort — then accomplishment within the organization is likely to be defined in terms of the dislodging of any chunk of that mass. The need to accomplish spending instead of rationing does not impart to an organization's members a sense of scarcity about the supply of funds. Decisions cannot help but be influenced by this absence of a sense of scarcity.

Money Moving

The bureaucratic jargon of the donor organization reflects the difficulty with which resources flow. In AID, for example, one hears talk about "moving money": how urgent it is to "move" a certain amount of funds within a limited time, how jubilant one is, after obtaining a loan authorization, at having "moved" so much money, how adept an administrator is at "moving" millions of dollars. At a farewell dinner for an AID administrator, the speaker praised the guest of honor for the major accomplishment of having "moved millions of dollars" during his stewardship at AID.

New loan officers are considered bright and energetic if they are good at moving money. Country mission directors, especially newly appointed ones, know they must move certain amounts of money in order to prove their worth and can distinguish themselves further by moving even more. I once expressed doubts to a recently appointed mission director about a proposed agricultural project which, although quite inventive, lacked the host government's participation and interest and did not have the support of the official entity which was supposed to administer it. He was fully aware of this problem, he said, but was determined to put the project through "this year," and was not going to "wait around" until the host government got interested. It is hard to consider such a course of action as irresponsible, if one is aware of (1) the real pressure to commit resources that is exerted on a donor organization from within and without and (2) the standards of individual employee performance within such a bureaucracy, which place high priority on the ability to move money.[4] A donor organization's sense of mission, then, relates not necessarily to economic development but to the commitment of resources, the moving of money. The individual knows that his career in the institution will be very much determined by his abilities in this area.[5]

The money-moving environment is not unique to development assistance entities. It is encountered in many bureaucracies funded by annual government appropriations.[6] Even if an agency does not lose the funds it is unable to use up by the end of the fiscal year, congressional appropriations committees will nevertheless consider such leftovers to be evidence that the agency does not need as much as it is asking for in subsequent budgets.[7] Hence the pressure to spend money during the course of the fiscal year, since one never knows if the natural rhythm of commitment will turn out to be slower than the annual rate of appropriation. Under such pressure, an agency's annual appropriation will inevitably be perceived by its employees as if it were a fixed source of supply with no alternative use — no opportunity cost — and hence no scarcity value. Indeed, such funds have *negative* opportunity costs in the sense that if the funds are not spent, the agency will incur "costs" in the form of problems with Congress the next time around.

AID had its own version of the end-of-the-fiscal-year rush. The amount of activity in Washington and the field missions increased considerably in the months preceding June 30. Washington prodded the field into hurrying up its loan papers and sent its technicians, if necessary, to help out. In the field, there was a flurry of meetings, phone calls to the borrower imploring him to complete his part of the documentation, and overtime work by secretaries and their bosses, with drafts of loan papers being fed to the typist page by page. Sometimes a mission would drag its feet on the preparation of a loan paper during the year and submit it to Washington strategically close to the June 30 deadline. A "desperate" Washington might give "less of a hard time" when reviewing the loan paper and asking for changes, because of the scarcity of staff review time caused by the last-minute increase in papers. Hence the chances for Washington approval of a problematic project might be greater during the pre-June 30 rush, when nonapproval of a project, or delay into the next fiscal year, had to be weighed against the cost of ending the year with uncommited funds.

The process of committing funds abroad entails much greater delay than spending them at home. For this reason, annual congressional reviews and appropriations hamper the administration of a foreign spending program to a greater extent than that of a domestic one. Because of this greater difficulty of committing funds smoothly, the pressure to move money in a foreign spending program is correspondingly greater than in domestic programs. The near impossibility of administering an intelligent foreign aid program on the basis of annual congressional reviews and appropriations has been recognized for some time. Since the late nineteen-fifties, foreign aid supporters have requested, to no avail, that appropriations for the U.S. aid program be authorized on a multi-year basis or that the program be given authority to borrow.

We know, then, that various forms of money-moving behavior exist in all annually and legislatively funded public institutions. It comes as quite a surprise, therefore, to find that the money-moving atmosphere of the U.S. aid program exists at the IBRD and IDB as well, despite the fact that these institutions are not annually beholden to an appropriation process. The two organizations, moreover, have engaged in an informal competition with each other for project borrowers in Latin America by offering concessions to the potential borrower on financing terms and encouraging their own technicians to help get the borrower before the other bank did.[8] Ironic, in a world of development assistance scarcity, but perfectly understandable in terms of the money-moving phenomenon. Indeed, some of the IBRD-IDB competition followed on the heels of announcements by both institutions that they would increase their lending significantly (a doubling by the IBRD, a 50 percent increase by the IDB).[9] To accomplish this desired leap forward in resource transfer, the IBRD doubled its professional staff in less than five years. Some of its long-term professionals, who prided themselves on belonging to a development assistance elite, complained about the remarkable increase in the number of new faces in the building, the mounting pressure to push projects through, and the possible sacrifice in the quality of bank decisionmaking. "The Bank is becoming like AID!" complained a project engineer, referring to the IBRD's traditional scorn for the quality of AID engineering and economic analysis. In the same vein, many AID technicians, who had transferred to the IBRD or IDB because of the increased level of activity of the latter entities compared to the decreased appropriations for the former, reported with surprise that the pressures to move money at these institutions were just as great as in the program from which they came.

In sum, the existence of money-moving behavior at the development assistance banks, as distinguished from the appropriation-tied U.S. aid program, makes the explanation of the phenomenon more difficult. It cannot be attributed to the fact that a government bureaucracy is appropriated a lump sum with the implicit admonition to get rid of it by the end of the year.

How Organizational Output Is Defined

Perhaps some clue to the explanation of the money-moving syndrome in development assistance entities, and the corollary absence of a sense of scarcity in decisionmaking, can be found in the standards by which development institutions judge their performance and are judged by the outside world. Whatever the reason, the single most desired and most noticed type of organizational performance relates to the quantitative estimates of aggregate needs for development assistance. How does the donor's contribution stand in relation to total estimated need, once the contribution of other suppliers is accounted for? How can the entity's share in total supply, and its contribution toward increasing that total, be dramatically increased? This quantitative standard of performance, and the often difficult-to-achieve target figure to which it is related, creates in the donor entities a type of self-pressure toward spending money that is just as effective as the continuous threat of congressional year-end questions about why a total appropriation could not be spent.

The estimates of total capital needs for development assistance in relation to supply seem to have been the implicit standard by which donor organizations have guided their behavior and judged their performance. The Pearson Report, as a typical example, suggests that the objective of development assistance ought to be related to "a global target rate of growth in GNP" for developing countries, from which the assistance requirement is deduced (page 124). Or, as put less sympathetically by an AID administrator in Southeast Asia, "The missing link in the development of the Third World was the 1 percent of the gross national product of industrialized nations."[10]

Any step toward increasing total supply of development assistance funds almost automatically qualifies as the right step. The organizational problems attending the transfer do not get much attention.[11] The insufficiency of total supply usually gets prime space in the reports on development problems, with discussions about why and how that supply should be increased, how the burden should be divided between countries, and what the best estimate of need might be.[12] By the same token, the announcements about development assistance that carry the most political impact and drama — excepting those related to scandal — have to do with significant increases or cutbacks in aggregate funds, rather than with the content of programs.

How has it happened that aggregate estimates of development assistance needs have come to play a primary role in the way development entities judge themselves and are judged by others? To some extent, the quantitative measure has gained its supremacy by default. Other definitions of success and failure of development assistance efforts have been hard to come by. The problem is not uncommon in other public sector money-spending programs where the difficulty of defining performance leaves a vacuum often filled by career concerns such as risk aversion. The problem of definition in development assistance is particularly acute because of the relatively short history of this sector of public finance, the underdeveloped nature of the literature in the field, and the location of development programs in faraway places.

Another reason for the overbearing presence of the total quantity benchmark is that the development assistance problem has usually been defined in terms of the relative insufficiency of the amount of funds supplied — just as most foreign policy problems have gravitated to definitions in terms of inadequate protection against the communist threat. Whether communist threat or inadequate total amounts, these were the definitions that produced results in terms of public support. People have been told that the development assistance problem is one of inadequate supply: this is how funds have been appropriated and otherwise raised, and this is the definition around which development administrators have fashioned their careers.

This is not to say that funds are adequate. Rather, the overshadowing of the organizational problem by the supply problem has kept people from recognizing the inability of the currently structured system — or the proposed streamlined versions of it — to accomplish the kind and amount of resource transfer needed.

Another cause, and perhaps effect, of the neglect of the organizational question is that the most respected economists who have turned their attention to development assistance have until recently focused on macroeconomic questions: the estimation of foreign exchange and savings gaps, the fiscal and monetary effects of assistance injections, the estimation of total needs for development assistance, and the effects of development assistance on the developing world's future foreign debt obligations.[13] The economic research unit of AID, with which some of these economists were associated for brief periods of time, also concentrated on this type of question. Research was never carried out, for example, on the effects on local industry of local versus foreign procurement, the demand-generating aspect of aid-financed public sector projects, the economic effects of aid-financed projects on the regions in which they were located, or other topics of this sort.

A notable exception to the development assistance economist's lack of attention to non-macroeconomic questions has been the economic research unit of the IBRD.[14] A major concern of this unit has been the application of shadow prices to project analyses as a way of correcting the capital and foreign exchange biases caused by the pricing of capital in these analyses at the artificially low terms of the IBRD loans. The bank's work in this area represents a significant contribution toward refinement of the techniques of project analysis and toward correction, for analytical purposes, of a distortion of the market mechanism caused by development lending itself.

The refined cost-benefit analysis still cannot reach a significant part of the distortion caused by the availability of development assistance for large projects with large foreign exchange components. The best that shadow price analysis can do is to select the best alternative from a group of projects that, on the average, are larger and have greater foreign exchange components than they would without the existence of a perceived foreign exchange abundance. As an IBRD economist said during a discussion of shadow pricing, "How do you calculate the shadow price of foreign exchange in comparing a hydro project with an equivalent thermal alternative when you know that the thermal plant — with its smaller foreign exchange component and lack of political appeal — has little chance of getting a loan in the first place?" Similarly, a Development Advisory Service economist wrote of his experience in Pakistan:

Not only are the shadow prices applied at the wrong end of the project planning process and by the wrong people, but they are also being applied to projects designed under an entirely different set of prices, the observed ones. By then it is too late to do much about the misallocation of resources. Even if directives are issued to the various agencies instructing them to use shadow prices in project design . . . scarcities still do not impinge on the agencies' proclivities.[15]

The highlighting of the total quantity problem and the corresponding overshadowing of the organizational problem makes it very difficult for a donor organization to recognize and examine openly the problems of its own structure and procedures; for such recognition involves a tacit admission by the organization that the reigning standard of maximum feasible transfer is not being met. It would be bad strategy, in short, for the organization to focus attention on the trouble it is having in making funds flow. This would defeat the attempt of assistance defenders to arouse a sense of public responsibility about the inadequacy of resources committed.

The license to reveal problems to the public as a way of gaining their support or of dispelling their misplaced criticism is quite important to the health of a public agency.[16] When the revelation to the·

public of private problems has value to an organization, the recognition and discussion of such problems *within* the institution will be facilitated. Where disclosure to the public is expected to have harmful effects, as in the case of the development assistance transfer problem, then this type of problem is not only concealed from outsiders but is also neglected in private. Instead of combating the outside world from its position of privileged inside knowledge, the entity ends up being invaded by the outside world's "misinformed" standards for determining progress and failure.

I have been trying to offer an explanation of why development assistance institutions and their members act in certain ways, rather than to show how they think or talk. Frequently, the argument focuses less on what people do, think, or say, than on what they do not do, do not think, and do not say. I have tried to find out why certain problems are not perceived as problems, rather than to argue that people or their institutions are aware of and ignore these problems. I have attempted to show that some inefficient decisionmaking occurs because of perfectly rational individual responses to organizational configurations —and not that decisions are made in ignorance, or despite knowledge that they contradict policy goals. Because people do not talk about certain things, certain problems do not get the kind of attention necessary to make them surface and demand resolution.

The Economic Analysis and Selection of Projects

We have seen so far that the generic slowness of transferring resources through present methods of project lending combined with the policy that limits development assistance to import costs have acted together to diminish the supply of projects available for development financing. This difficulty in generating a flow of financeable projects, in turn, has had negative repercussions on the status of economic criteria in the design and selection of projects.

Economic analysis thrives on scarcity, on the need to ration resources in scarce supply among competing claims. When competing claims do not exist and funds are not perceived as scarce, then the economist's skill is no longer functional. The administrator is not dependent on him to find out how to ration, in the way that he (the administrator) *is* dependent on the engineer to tell him the best location for a dam. Even where there is little sense of resource scarcity, however, one finds that the economist's services are sought increasingly by public entities. He is still needed to help his agency, not necessarily to make decisions, but to get projects approved. For in the world of project approval and raising of funds, development capital is *supposed* to be scarce, and thus projects are *supposed* to meet economic criteria. Yet when alternatives are few or nonexistent in institutional reality, then economic criteria can have no more force than the moral injunction to be good: one "ought" to avoid economic misallocation, even though one does not have to. Needless to say, the moral imperative to be economic can have little punch in a world where the most compelling absolute is that money shall be spent.[17]

The foregoing explains in part why so much economic analysis of projects in development assistance and other public sector entities either amounts to a *post hoc* rationalization of decisions already taken, or is not allowed to focus on the relevant alternatives, and hence almost always comes out in favor of the project in hand. As a participant in Pakistani development decisions wrote: "First the technical people design the project, then the economists and planners evaluate it. The technical agencies formulate the scheme according to their lights, and it returns to the planning authority as a finished project report. Then the planners set about the work of evaluation. At this stage, they are faced with a virtual *fait accompli*."[18] In such cases economic analysis is facilitating increased bureaucratic output by helping get projects approved, rather than showing how to allocate scarce resources.

The recognition of the second-class position of economics in decisions regarding project design and approval underlies the frequent recommendation of evaluators that techniques of economic analysis be improved to fit developing-country contexts and that criteria of economic fitness be more rigorously imposed inside donor organizations. While such analytical improvement always helps, it does not affect the second-class citizenship of the economist. It does not change him from an annoying moral preacher to a scientific knower. In the attempt to bestow first-class status on economic considerations, the most refined techniques of analysis cannot substitute for a setting in which development financing looks scarce and competing claims abundant, from within the organization's walls.

In a way, I am saying that the slowness of project lending flows is not caused by rigorous project evaluation but by the nature of the task at hand, the organizational traits of the entities carrying out the task, and the constraints within which these entities must work. Thoroughness in this case is not necessarily the cause of slowness, but in a certain sense is the *result* of it. The delay of present transfer methods, one might say, has allowed for the time-consuming luxury of rigorous evaluation in a manner somewhat reminiscent of Parkinson's Law.[19] As if to complete a vicious circle, the poor quality of bureaucratic output resulting from the difficulties of transfer has generated the demand for increased rigor in economic analysis and selection of projects. Rigor, then, seems to have become just as much an extension of bureaucratic delay and complexity as a source of improvement of the quality of decisionmaking.[20]

This reasoning cuts across the traditional dichotomy of slowness/thoroughness versus haste/waste. This is because the perception of capital abundance within donor organizations relates not to absolute amounts of capital needed and supplied but to the *rate* at which these amounts are supplied and demanded through time. A speeded-up resource transfer — brought about, for example, by a larger supply of projects — might lessen the distorted perception of capital as relatively abundant, and hence eliminate one source of the inefficient decisionmaking emanating from the donor world.

I do not recommend the abandonment of rigor in economic analysis. Rather, I am suggesting that the rigor now existing — and the increased amounts of it recommended in the official reports — is not completely genuine. Too much of the burden for producing good-quality bureaucratic output is placed on the technology of analyzing and screening project proposals. Some of this burden could be transferred to the incentives and disincentives which influence the actions of the donor organizations and operate independently of the screening technology. Such a shifting of the burden would not only facilitate an improvement in the quality of development assistance but would be likely to turn techniques of analysis into more effective instruments of bureaucratic production than they are now.

AVOIDING ABUNDANCE

Program lending can be seen as an attempt to get around the abundance problem, though it usually is not justified that way (see page 57 above). By significantly reducing the number of decisions to be made per dollar transferred, the program loan seems to have the potential for eliminating abundance decisionmaking. It changes the lending decision from a microeconomic one to a macroeconomic one, depending on sweeping judgments about the country's economic performance or potential and its political performance. Hence the program loan decision has more political weight and visibility and is taken at a higher level in the organization than the decision to finance a project. This type of loan decision, one would think, would lie outside the environment of abundance and not be subject to its perverse economic incentives. The mechanism runs into different problems, however, precisely because of the high-level and politically significant intrusion into recipient-country governing that it occasions.[21]

It was the political difficulties of program lending that led two of its critics to propose another mechanism for development transfers.[22] The Hirschman-Bird tax credit proposal would have allowed individual taxpayers a credit to invest in the developing country and project of their choice. Although the proposal was designed as an antidote to program lending problems, it can also be seen as a direct onslaught on the organizational problems of project lending. It resolves the organizational problem by circumventing it: the individual's choice in the "free market" of projects and countries completely replaces the distorted "prices" of the organizational world in determining who gets what. The organizational apparatus suggested by the authors to administer the program, however, looks just as vulnerable to the problems described here. The tax credit proposal and program loan mechanism, in sum, suggest the kind of approach that might make inroads into the organizational problem in development assistance. Unfortunately, the two approaches have their own serious failings, which cancel out their potential for curing the organizational problem.

One may ask, at this point, why the organizational problem cannot be cured immediately with the economist's swift and powerful stroke: the return of allocational decisionmaking to its proper place in the free market. After all, that solution was hinted at in my description of the tax credit proposal. Much of the bad decisionmaking decribed until now, that is, should be curable by raising the price of development assistance capital to its scarcity value and letting the market take over the decisionmaking. From this point of view, it is the subsidized price of development lending, rather than policy or organizational variables, that is causing the problems of too much equipment, too many imports, and projects that are too big. Indeed, it was the recognition that this subsidized price was causing distortions which led the IBRD to introduce such correctives as shadow pricing the cost of capital, labor, and foreign exchange in cost-benefit analyses, or insisting that loan covenants for revenue-earning projects guarantee the charging of rates that will cover costs.[23] These measures were meant to carry the burden of ensuring efficient allocations of development capital, in lieu of a nonsubsidized price for that capital. Such techniques could be seen, however, as an elaborate and ineffective way of getting at an allocational inefficiency that might have been easily eliminated with a simple "liberation" of price.

It has been argued, in the same vein, that the availability of sub-sidized development capital makes it less likely that developing countries will confront the inadequacies of their own financial markets, thus creating a vicious cycle of foreign assistance and financial underdevelopment. McKinnon suggests that foreign assistance in the form of a purchasing market for market-priced recipient-country securities might help break this cycle and its corresponding dependency. It would decentralize assistance decisionmaking by taking it right out of the organization and putting it into the hands of the recipient-country entrepreneurs, where it should function most efficiently.[24]

Is this where the logic of my argument is leading? No, and for the same reason that my analysis of development assistance does not center on the price charged for it. The price analysis of the development assistance problem, though of considerable value, tells us little about the organizational forms of dealing with allocational decisions. The organization, in such analyses, is a passive being through which the market transmits its signals, functioning as invisibly as price — as in the tax credit scheme. By the same token, the organization is not very apparent in the above-described scheme for liberating development assistance prices from their subsidized levels. The proposal suggests that recipient-country public institutions, for example, could spread risks by providing guarantees on debt issues by domestic enterprises, thereby expediting a flow of development assistance portfolio capital. These guarantees could be provided to "borrowers whose viability and contribution to development had been thoroughly researched."[25] The selection and "thorough researching" of the borrower, however, implies a very visible organizational entity making decisions that are, by definition, outside the marketplace. In this price approach to the question, then, the organization appears only dimly through a parenthetical clause and a passive voice. In my analysis, the organization is as central and potent a character as price.

I do not deny the power of the analytical lens of price. My own organizational discussion is shot through with the determinism of price-like signals. Nevertheless, the free-market-price solution of this problem leaves things incomplete,[26] as do the remedies proposed at the beginning of this volume. The concluding argument of the next chapter should clarify better why this is so.

CONCLUSION

What would happen if development assistance entities financed foreign and local costs, without discrimination, in their project loans? This proposal, by the way, was made twenty years ago by IBRD economists precisely on the grounds that it would help move money.[27] As the result of such a change, of course, money-moving behavior would not disappear. Projects would continue to tend toward bigness, because of administrative scale economies, and projects that otherwise might be considered marginal would continue to be financed. Removing the constraint, nevertheless, would have important positive effects, since the policy of financing only imports feeds and strengthens the phenomenon of money-moving. Imported equipment, for example, would lose the "cheapness" it now has, and the tendency to import rather than buy locally would not be encouraged to such an extent. Even though capital extravagance caused by money-moving would continue, the extension of the extravagance to local costs would represent a significant advantage over the current system since it would mean an increase for local industry of the particularly growth-stimulating type of demand that is characteristic of public sector investment programs. This result, at the least, is consistent with the goals of development assistance. The capital extravagance that now takes place, in contrast, hinders the development efforts of local industry in the recipient country. If one is stuck with money-moving decisionmaking, then, the nondiscriminating form of capital extravagance may be less bad than the current discriminating one.

To look upon local costs with the same favor as foreign ones might also give more chance to the labor-using choices discussed above. In fact, the donor world has expressed considerable concern about the capital bias of its choices and the income-regressive development paths of many of its recipients. This concern has led not to a reconsideration of the import-cost policy, but to a strong emphasis on income distribution and employment problems in recipient countries. The donor world has made a considerable effort during the nineteen-seventies to retool itself for lending in agriculture, health, and education — sectors in which the possibilities for large, equipment-intensive projects happen to be not as great. But if donor organizations were not able to take advantage of the myriad labor-using opportunities in, for example, highway lending,[28] then they may be no better able to meet the challenge in these other sectors. As the evidence has shown, capital emphases are quite possible in these sectors, though they may not be as glaring: tractors instead of simpler implements, imported tubewells instead of simpler local ones, school buildings without teachers, educational television equipment.[29] The new bias, then, and the extensive research and adaptation that goes along with it, may turn out to be a tortuous and unproductive way of trying to get at developing-country reality. Abandoning the practice of financing mainly foreign exchange costs might have been a less complicated antidote to the capital bias, even though the money-moving causes of big-project financing would still remain.

Interestingly, the attempt of donor organizations to shift from a capital to a labor bias is, like similar shifts before it, a response to problems posed mainly within the confines of the donor world. Only peripherally did the recipient country participate in this learning process and change of heart, playing instead the role of responder to trends in development thinking. To the extent that the new concern for income distribution was born outside the mistakes and struggles of the developing world, then, it may not "take" very well.

Perhaps it is not fair or accurate to present the new income distribution moves of the donor world in such a cold light. Much of the change was inspired by a genuine concern with income inequalities and the seeming lack of progress in this area. Radical politics in the developed world, moreover, brought donor organizations under attack for financing status quo governments and abetting social stagnation. Finally, the new concern with income distribution represents a commendable ability to learn from past experience, an admission of some ignorance about how development occurs, and a vow to find out more about it. Applying the theory of unbalanced growth to organizations instead of economies, one could say that the new concern for income distribution represents an organizational reaction to an "excess supply" of capital emphases in the past. In this light, both the bias of the past and that of the present might be explained as the normal dynamics of healthy organizational growth.

The temptations of capital-intensive bigness may be so irresistible in transport, power, and other infrastructure projects that abstinence from these sectors will turn out to be a good thing. The new and avid devotion to employment-creation and the less dazzling opportunities for capital bias in agriculture, education, and health may together be strong enough to turn the tide against the continuing large-project biases of the organizational environment. At the same time, it is difficult to see how a directive to pursue labor-using strategies can be as powerful in guiding choices as an organizational setting which continues to emit strong signals in favor of large, capital-intensive projects. Even if the policy of financing mainly imports were removed, the organizational environment described in this chapter would live on.

Chapter Eight

CONCLUSION

In the preceding chapter, it was seen that the overly large project was a rational organizational response to the way a development assistance organization's output was defined. At the same time, this response was out of keeping with the organization's development-promoting purposes and resulted in inefficient choices. Similarly, it was seen in chapter 6 that it was perfectly rational for the borrower country, in confronting the foreign assistance scene, to make resource allocation decisions as if foreign exchange were abundant in relation to domestic resources. This perception led to inefficient uses of scarce resources — which was one of the problems that development assistance was supposed to ameliorate. Again, it was seen in chapter 4 that the U.S. foreign aid agency was perfectly reasonable in giving high priority to U.S. export promotion in its decisionmaking because this approach was basic to its survival in the institutional world of the federal government. At the same time, this priority was directly contradictory to the foreign aid objective of promoting private sector development in the borrower country. Finally, it was seen in chapter 3 that decentralization was a fitting organizational approach to a task like development assistance. At the same time, decentralization made alienation from the borrower-country environment functional. In short, inadequacies of development assistance programs could be understood as the results of rational organizational responses to the assistance task and task environment. What made sense for the or-

102

ganization contravened its objectives.

True, development assistance performance also reflected policies and political pressures impinging on the organization from without — such as the outside criticism discussed in chapter 4 and the policy of financing only import costs discussed in chapter 6. But these other forces might have been contained if the organizational factors discussed in this volume had not propelled assistance programs in the same problematic direction. These organizational dilemmas make it difficult to conceive of a development assistance organization along current or proposed lines that would be able to carry out its task without generating the elements of its own unsatisfactory performance.

Much of the organizational behavior described in this volume is of a type that private firms engage in to gain control over uncertain task environments. These organizations do certain things, that is, when faced with a high degree of uncertainty in the world from which they get their inputs or into which they sell their outputs.[1] As the study of private firms has shown, organizations try to gain control over parts of uncertain task environments by bringing their random occurrences within the realm of forecasting predictability. Control may be gained by creating a new organization out of that uncertain environment — that is, by integrating vertically. This vertical extension into the environment outside an organization is considered most desirable when the technology of the product is "long linked, with each activity dependent on the one preceding it and providing a needed input to the one following."[2]

In development assistance, one of the highly uncertain elements of the organization's task environment is the beneficiary's input, as pointed out in chapter 4. The erratic nature of this supply can be highly disruptive of the organization's "production process," leading to the tendency for public sector project generation to be transferred from the borrower government to the lending institution. This taking over of project generation by development assistance institutions is like the backward vertical integration of firms in the private sector. The organization expands "backward" into the task environment and starts to "manufacture" project applications itself. It thereby lessens the high degree of uncertainty of the environment from which it must get its inputs, assuring itself of a more reliable source of supply.

During the nineteen-sixties, for example, the IBRD made certain policy changes in favor of financing pre-investment or feasibility studies. This extension of its activities beyond capital project financing "evolved out of its interest in finding and financing projects that it could regard as technically sound, economically viable, and of high priority for the developing country."[3] These policy changes can also be seen as an attempt to gain some control over the institutional mechanism by which inputs are made. Indeed, it was not only the uncertainty of the recipient-country environment which the bank was seeking to diminish by such a move; it was also the uncertainty of the already established procedures for generating feasibility studies in the *developed* world — mainly, the UNDP. What was originally conceived of as a rational division of labor between donor organizations — feasibility studies taken care of by the UNDP and investment by the IBRD — turned out to be unworkable for the latter organization because of the importance for its production process of a smooth flow of one of its major inputs, project applications. The UNDP's preinvestment studies, that is, were considered by the IBRD as "almost totally devoid of the financial data and analyses that are needed for [an] investment decision."[4] The IBRD, in sum, moved in the direction of backward vertical integration in order to increase its control over the supply of projects submitted to it.

Program loans can also be seen as an attempt to reduce uncertainty. By agreeing on a fiscal and monetary program with the borrower country and reviewing that program along the way, the donor organization reduces uncertainty about whether the product can be "sold." The organization also puts itself in a better position to judge whether this particular consumer will be qualified to come back another time for more. By taking actions akin to forward integration, then, the assistance entity gains greater control over the smooth disposal of its product and, in the bargain, engineers a greater number of "bulk" sales.

Another contingency-reducing action taken by a donor organization was the IBRD's strong emphasis on the creation of autonomous agencies, or mixed companies, to carry out and administer the public sector projects it financed in recipient countries. The mixed company, it was said, would be more financially sound and businesslike.[5] At the same time, however, this organizational form represented an attempt to reduce the difficulties of an uncertain task environment by integrating "forward," for a mixed company could be more responsive than a government ministry to the standards of the donor organization. The existence of the mixed company as loan "consumer" increased the probability that funds would be properly used and the project well run.

The large project provides the donor organization with a control very similar to that of the mixed company. In addition to the organizational economies discussed in the last chapter, the large project also provides more certainty over the "sale" of the organization's product. Just as the mixed company centralizes decisionmaking in one group of people, the big project centralizes project activity in one place. Just as the mixed company is organizationally separate from the rest of government, so the big project is usually physically separate from what is happening in the rest of the country. An IBRD report on labor-intensive methods for highway construction projects cited as a disadvantage of such methods the inability to contain project activity in one place. "Unlike dam construction," it said, "where work is concentrated in one place for several years, road construction camps must be moved every 3-4 months; this is much more expensive for a large labor force than for a few pieces of equipment."[6] The big project, of course, was never explicitly justified on such grounds, even though the preference for mixed companies was. Both forms, however, provide the same benefits of self-containedness and insulation.

The policy of financing only import costs can also be understood in terms of the quest for certainty over the sale of one's product. To the extent that foreign exchange costs are embodied in tangible goods rather than services, they can be seen with the eye and are therefore more amenable to control. To the extent, moreover, that these foreign exchange funds finance equipment imports rather than other intermediate goods, there will be more expenditure accounted for by a given physical volume; one glance will be able to encompass more of the financing. "This emphasis on equipment financing," wrote the IBRD in justifying its handling of the highway maintenance problem with equipment loans, "meant relatively quick disbursement of loan funds and limited project supervision problems."[7] Even if the financed imports are services from the donor world, they are more controllable than recipient-country services through the better grasp one has of the workings of the institutions of one's own culture. The policy of financing imports, then, makes sense in terms of the need for control over the flow of a product out of the organization. Like the control provided by the big project, the financing of imports increases certainty for the donor organization at the same time that it contributes to the bigness and capital intensity of projects.

All these instances of contingency reduction have been justified by
donor organizations on other grounds: the financing of pre-
investment studies was meant to train recipients in the ways of
planning and to increase the absorptive capacity of the recipient
country; program loans would tie development assistance more
closely to a country's economic performance; the creation of mixed
companies would assure the lending institution that expensive capital projects financed by them would be administered by competent
groups which were organizationally less vulnerable to political
meddling; the policy of financing mainly foreign exchange costs
seemed the most efficient way to administer an assistance program
and also induced recipient countries to raise their own financing. The
spirit of these justifications is best summed up by an official of the
World Bank:

In the preparation of a large number of lending operations it was soon
discovered that governments . . . found it difficult to meet the domestic
investment expenditures even when the Bank was ready to finance the
foreign exchange cost. Therefore it had to take an interest in the fiscal
performance of borrowing governments, in the financial operations of
revenue-yielding projects and in attempts to supplement fiscal revenues
through borrowing operations by governments and government agencies.[8]

All these explanations, of course, have their own validity. They
must also be recognized, however, as attempts to gain some control
over an extremely difficult task environment by *incorporating* parts of
it. At this point, the analogy to the private firm's solution to an
uncertain task environment runs into trouble; the environment that
one is shaping into a reliable supplier of inputs, or consumer of
outputs, is another country. This shaping is likely to involve the
destiny of a whole sector of that country's economy. It may attach to
the economy a certain development strategy that, though best for
reducing donor-organization uncertainty, will hinder the pursuit of
development.

The creation of a mixed company, for example, may not always be
the most desirable choice when investigating a certain sector. It has
been argued, for example, that a decentralized decisionmaking apparatus in agriculture might result in better choices than the centralization involved in creating a single company:

A common response of World Bank and other donor agencies [to the problem
of unsatisfactory performance of government field staff in agriculture at the
local level] has been to rely on administrative arrangements aimed at by-
passing the problem. Thus, the implementation of aid-financed projects

frequently involves the creation of a semiautonomous organization, usually with a considerable complement of foreign experts, rather than relying on existing field organizations. . . . It is plausible to argue, however, that agricultural development objectives could be advanced much more effectively by measures to raise the level of performance of the existing organizations and field staff.[9]

Such decentralization may be more likely to produce agricultural development projects that are in harmony with the human and physical resource endowments of a given region. A decentralized field organization may also be more likely to avoid labor-displacing decisions or to recognize and deal with labor displacement as it occurs. On the one hand, then, centralization of investment activity in a mixed company provides certainty and control for the donor organization. On the other hand, it can result in choices that are wrong not only for the economy involved but for the goals of the donor program itself.

The recent literature in agricultural development has argued that organizational or geographical decentralization is often more compatible with project choices that are labor-using — in short, it is more in harmony with the new emphases of the donor world in employment creation and income redistribution. A study of a rural works program in Indonesia shows how decentralized decisionmaking on specific projects accounted for much of the success of the program. The nature of employment problems was seasonal and there were "joint benefits to be derived from labor-intensive rural investments."[10] Another study pointed out that non-foodgrain agricultural commodities, which play an important role in consumption as incomes rise, have received suprisingly little attention in development plans. "Many of these products are highly labour intensive. . . . The production opportunities are often broadly diffused geographically, facilitating a regional balance in labour use."[11] A study of agricultural equipment in India and Pakistan suggested that the redesigning of relatively sophisticated equipment into simpler forms could significantly reduce the necessity for joint action by farmers and thus make this technology more accessible to small farmers.[12] A study of agricultural employment possibilities in developing countries recommended the decentralization of agricultural research as the only way to get research organizations to come up with location-specific crop recommendations and technologies. In general, as the latter study points out, more decentralized efforts may often be the only way to make labor-intensive schemes work.[13] Decentralization, then, is one kind of program design that might help a donor organization further its new goals. Yet the organization may not be able to avail itself of this alternative because of its need to gain certainty over its environment.

The priority now being given by the donor world to employment and income distribution problems is, in a sense, a grand design for changing the kind of history described in this volume. Yet a whole array of already-existing approaches to the problem may be out of reach because of the primacy of the organizational quest for certainty in the task environment. This need may preclude project designs that are decentralized; that finance costs of labor or costs complementary to it; that finance local costs; that involve many small projects rather than one larger one; and that involve projects stretched over time and space rather than concentrated at one point. An observer of agricultural development assistance in East Africa writes an excellent summary of the problem:

> Planners have been preoccupied with capital and development expenditure, with capital projects and with the creation of special project organizations, to the relative neglect of recurrent expenditure and of programmes which are implemented through existing field organizations. This preoccupation may originate in part from the bias of aid agencies towards financial aid tied to capital inputs; in part from the relative ease with which an economist can carry out his professional activities with a capital project compared with the difficulties of handling poor or missing data for a recurrent resource project (or, more typically, a programme of rather small individual projects); in part from the policy of some donor agencies, most conspicuously the IBRD, of preferring to ensure effective operation in the recipient country by creating a semi-autonomous organization rather than risking operation through existing field organizations; and in part from the attraction of the more visible single, large "project" compared with the less visible dispersed field "programme."[14]

The search for employment and income-distribution strategies, then, may be doomed to run up against the organization's more basic impulses to function smoothly. At the least, the new concern for employment and income distribution should be recognized as, to some extent, an attempt of the donor world to escape its own organizational constraints, and not only as a search for knowledge where there is none.

Since development assistance involves countries, not companies, there will be political constraints to the backward and forward expansion of donor organizations. Incorporation of parts of one's surroundings beyond certain limits is not politically feasible, no matter how much the organization needs to reduce the uncertainty of the world

around it. The attempts of a donor organization to better control its
environment will come to look like, or even turn into, the imperialistic behavior of a developed country. Whether or not development
assistance is inspired or subverted by imperialistic motives, the logic
of the organizational scene will, on its own, lead the assistance entity
to look *as if* it were acting that way.

This organizational logic does not only lead to an explanation of
"imperialistic" activity by donor organizations. It also throws light
on the dependency problem of Third World countries. Dependency
results from the fact that decisions affecting a nation's destiny are
frequently made outside its borders, usually by multinational corpor-
ations. In terms of my analysis, the inability of donor organizations to
live with uncertainty in their task environment also leads to dependency on the part of recipient countries. That is, the more that donor
organizations are able to impose order on the outside decisionmaking
that affects their product, the better they can perform their task. In so
doing, however, they bring dependency to those whose decisionmaking has been so ordered. Seen in this light, dependency is the
result not necessarily of design but of an organization's attempts to do
well. The difficulties that organizations have in living with certain
types of outside uncertainty, then, can be seen as leading to the worst
of both worlds: imperialistic behavior on one side of the donor-
recipient exchange, and a state of dependency on the other.

The development assistance organization, in sum, cannot help but
look at the recipient world as an uncertain environment to be mas-
tered through vertical integration. But this is the same world that the
developing country sees as the stage for its own development. What is
uncertainty to the donor organization is sovereignty to the borrower
country. What is an intolerably slow pace of beneficiary input to
project generation for the donor organization is, for the recipient
country, the groping that is normal to the process of growth. In short,
the space needed by a developing country to grapple with and take
charge of its destiny is turned into anathema for the donor organization, simply because that organization is dependent on the beneficiary world for a smooth flow of inputs and outputs.

When one looks at the development assistance problem in this way,
the key to its resolution seems obvious: what is needed is a setting in
which the uncertainty of the recipient world does not threaten the
organizational health of the donor entity. If donor organizations could
somehow gain independence from the pace and quality of recipient

government activity, then they would not be so compelled to impose their order on that world. The breaking of this strong organizational need for control would not merely diminish the expansionist tendencies of assistance activity. Such a change would also cut recipient-country decisionmaking loose from much of its developed-world bias and eliminate some of the costs to developing countries of exploring homegrown approaches.

My solution is simple only in terms of its logic. More difficult is the task of thinking up organizational or national relationships that would fit the qualifications set forth here and, at the same time, allow a substantial transfer of development capital. Though this task is difficult, it should be noted that my conclusions about development assistance are not as pessimistic as those ascribing its inadequacies to imperialist determinism. The latter say that the donor world needs the recipient world in order to maintain its own rate of growth. According to this logic, any assistance attempts by the donor world will be guided by that need to expand, no matter how noble the professed motives. My analysis, in contrast, allows for the possibility that the professed motives may be genuine, and that what gets in the way is an institutional framework that impels the organization to get better control over its environment. I ascribe problem results to an organizational, rather than a historical, determinism. One hopes that the former would be more subject to enlightened manipulation than the latter.

NOTES

CHAPTER I: INTRODUCTION

1. These included: *U.S. Foreign Assistance in the 1970's: A New Approach* (The Peterson Report), Report to the President from the Task Force on International Development (Washington, D.C.: GPO, 1970); Nelson A. Rockefeller, *The Rockefeller Report on the Americas*, The Official Report of a United States Presidential Mission for the Western Hemisphere (Chicago: Quadrangle Books, 1969); United Nations Development Programme, *A Study of the United Nations Development System* (The Jackson Report) (Geneva: United Nations, 1969).

2. For example, Raymond F. Mikesell, *The Economics of Foreign Aid* (Chicago: Aldine, 1968); Robert E. Asher, *Development Assistance in the Seventies: Alternatives for the United States* (Washington, D.C.: The Brookings Institution, 1970); Joan M. Nelson, *Aid, Influence, and Foreign Policy* (New York: Macmillan Co., 1968); John Pincus, *Trade, Aid and Development: The Rich and Poor Nations* (New York: McGraw-Hill, 1967); Teresa Hayter, *Aid As Imperialism* (Baltimore: Penguin Books, 1971); Jerome Levinson and Juan de Onis, *The Alliance That Lost Its Way* (Chicago: Quadrangle Books, 1970); Paul G. Clark, *American Aid for Development* (New York: Praeger, 1972); David Wall, *The Charity of Nations: The Political Economy of Foreign Aid* (New York: Basic Books, 1973).

3. I am following the popular and incorrect usage of "ugly American." The term comes from a book by that name, which depicts a foreign aid technician who was just the opposite of what we have come to think of as an "ugly American." See William J. Lederer and Eugene Burdick, *The Ugly American* (New York: Norton, 1958).

4. William K. Dill first used the expression "task environment" to specify those parts of the environment which were "relevant or potentially relevant to goal setting and goal attainment" by the organization. See "Environment as an Influence on Managerial Autonomy," *Administrative Science Quarterly* 2 (March 1958): 409-43, as cited in James D. Thompson, *Organizations in Action: Social Science Bases of Administrative Theory* (New York, McGraw-Hill, 1967), p. 27. I was assisted in thinking through the organizational analysis by Thompson's *Organizations in Action* and by Paul R. Lawrence and Jay W. Lorsch, *Organization and Environment: Managing Differentiation and Integration* (Boston: Graduate School of Business Administration, Harvard University, 1967), chapter 8.

5. Examples of this type of analysis are Anthony Downs, *Inside Bureaucracy* (Boston: Little, Brown and Company, 1966), chapter 17; or the case study of TVA by Philip Selznick, *TVA and the Grass Roots: A Study in the Sociology of Formal Organizations* (1949; reprint ed., New York: Harper Torchbooks, 1966).

6. Frederick Mosher points out similar shortcomings in the prevailing criticism of the State Department's Foreign Service: "There is a good deal of agreement in the nature of the criticisms[of the Service]. They include alleged lack of responsiveness, inertia, resistance to change, emphasis upon form and process rather than substance, insufficient specialization, red tape, over-conformism, inflexibility, lack of innovative thinking and initiative — *in short, most of the popularly accepted shortcomings of the bureaucracy*," ("Some Observations about Foreign Service Reforms: 'Famous First Words,' " *Public Administration Review* 29[November-December 1969]: 602).

7. Downs, *Inside Bureaucracy*, p. 204. His chapter 16 discusses the conditions under which innovation and receptivity to change may occur.

8. In addition to the literature cited above, see particularly Edward S. Mason and Robert E. Asher, *The World Bank Since Bretton Woods* (Washington, D.C.: The Brookings Institution, 1973); Sidney Dell, *The Inter-American Development Bank: A Study in Development Financing* (New York: Praeger, 1972); John White, *Regional Development Banks: The Asian, African and Inter-American Banks* (New York: Praeger, 1972).

9. Data are for the fiscal years 1967 and 1974. IBRD data are from *Annual Report*, 1974, and include credits of the International Development Association (IDA), the soft loan window of the IBRD. U.S. data are for economic assistance and are from U.S., Congress, Appropriations, *Foreign Assistance and Related Agencies, Appropriations for 1974*, part 2, Hearings Before the Subcommittee on Foreign Operations and Related Agencies, 93d Cong., 1st sess., 10 June 1973, p. 88; 1974 appropriation figure from U.S., Congress, House of Representatives, Committee on Appropriations, *Foreign Assistance and Related Programs, Appropriations for 1975*, 94th Cong., 1st sess., H. Rep. 94-53; AID personnel data from U.S., Congress, House Committee on Appropriations, *Foreign Assistance and Related Agencies, Appropriations for 1975*, part 2, Hearings Before the Subcommittee on Foreign Operations and Related Agencies, 93d Cong., 2d sess., 3 June 1974, p. 240.

10. Program loan expenses were $235 million out of $4,314 million. See IBRD, *Annual Report*, 1974.

11. House Committee on Appropriations, *Foreign Assistance and Related Agencies, Appropriations for 1975*, part 2, pp. 131, 168.

CHAPTER II: THE TASK AND THE ORGANIZATIONAL FIT

1. See, for example, *Personnel for the New Diplomacy* (The Herter Report), Report of the Committee on Foreign Affairs Personnel (Washington, D.C.: Carnegie Endowment for International Peace, 1962), p. 117.

2. "There is no need," George Foster writes, "to teach the average professional student to think first of identifying major problems and then working out solutions to these problems. The major problems are thought to be quite obvious; the need is to ameliorate, not to identify, them. The professional knows the kinds of questions his society will ask of him and the job demands it will make upon him. . . . Consequently, most professional training is designed in terms of *programs rather than underlying problems*" (*Traditional Cultures and the Impact of Technological Change* [New York: Harper & Row, 1962], pp. 178-79).

3. In the field of public administration, for example, Esman and Montgomery recommended that future ventures in technical cooperation "concentrate on experimental activities *for which there are no readily available standard solutions*, in which the United States and local participants can engage in solving important developmental problems through a cooperative learning process" (Milton J. Esman and John D. Montgomery, "Systems Approach to Technical Cooperation," *Public Administration Review* 29 [September-October 1969]: 514). Italics mine.

4. For instance: "Technical assistance transfers skills and knowledge" (Nelson, *Aid, Influence and Foreign Policy*, p. 7); "Technical assistance may be directed towards . . . an immediate increase in the stock of skills, by providing 'experts' who will do operational jobs" (Angus Maddison, *Foreign Skills and Technical Assistance in Economic Development* [Paris: Development Centre of the Organisation for Economic Co-operation and Development, 1965], pp. 12-13, as quoted in Mason and Asher, *World Bank Since Bretton Woods*).

5. Discomfort with the "transfer concept" of development know-how is also expressed in *A Study of the Capacity of the United Nations Development System* (The Jackson Report), vol. 2, p. 164.

6. Thompson, *Organizations in Action*, p. 10.

7. As a way of confronting this problem in the area of technical assistance, an ex-administrator of AID suggested that the innovating function be organizationally

separate from the operational part of the program. "As an operating organization, AID has understandably emphasized the application of existing technical knowledge, recruitment of career managerial and operating personnel, and technical assistance activities with reasonably assured pay-offs. AID has been weakest, therefore, in sponsoring coherent and cumulative research activities, in attracting specialized professional personnel, in building working relations with U.S. professional communities, and in undertaking high-potential but high-risk experiments in technical assistance. Thus, it seems to me, there is a valid case for making some special arrangements to encourage greater innovation in technical assistance. . . . The most rational grounds for separating an Institute from the proposed Corporation is this distinction between innovating and operating functions" (Clark, *American Aid for Development*, pp. 185, 187).

8. Tom Burns and G. M. Stalker, *The Management of Innovation* (London: Tavistock Publications, 1961) as cited in Lawrence and Lorsch, *Organization and Environment*, pp.187-88. See also Thompson, *Organizations in Action*, p. 143; James Q. Wilson, "Innovation in Organization: Notes Toward a Theory," in *Approaches to Organizational Design*, ed. James D. Thompson (Pittsburgh: University of Pittsburgh Press, 1966), pp. 200-201; Harold Leavitt, "Unhuman Organizations," *Harvard Business Review* 40 (July-August 1962): 90-98, as cited in *Organization and Environment*, pp. 199-201.

9. Michel Crozier goes so far as to argue that "the freedom and discretion of the innovator figure require the strict ritualism of the petty officials and the submissiveness of the middle officials if they are to develop fully" (*The Bureaucratic Phenomenon* [Chicago: University of Chicago Press, Phoenix Books, 1967], p. 202). Italics mine.

10. In the study of the State Department Foreign Service Officers, the decentralized familylike unit was also considered to have an influence on behavior. "The respondents suggested that the younger the individual, the further away from Washington, the smaller the embassy (up to a certain point) and then the more informal the embassy, the less the tendency to view type A behavior as competent behavior" (Chris Argyris, "Some Causes of Organizational Ineffectiveness within the Department of State," Center for International Systems Research, Occasional Paper no. 2 [Washington, D.C.: Department of State, 1966], p. 17). (Type A behavior was characterized as retreating from the aggressiveness or hostility of oneself or others, refraining from open expression of positive or negative feelings, accepting dependence upon others, especially under conditions of risk-taking, etc.)

11. "There is an almost feudal quality about the relationship between the senior and the lower ranks in the mission which is not only out of keeping with the democratic character of American life, but is also a strong deterrent to creativity. The degree of subservience traditionally accorded to the Ambassador and his wife and the degree of control exercised by them over the private lives of their subordinates . . . is in almost all cases such that only the most courageous officers will feel that they can differ openly with the Chief of Mission" (U.S., Department of State, "Task Force VII, Stimulation of Creativity," in *Diplomacy for the 70's: A Program of Management Reform for the Department of State*, Department of State Publication 8551, Department and Foreign Service Series no. 143, pp. 333-34.

12. Moreover, AID rotation procedures were less arbitrary than those of the Foreign Service in that the employee had more of a say in whether and where he wanted to go.

13. To illustrate: AID's Foreign Service Reserve officers, when recruited from other government agencies, are specifically forbidden the right of reinstatement in their original agency in the same, corresponding, or higher position upon termination of their employment in AID. This right is guaranteed to State Department Foreign Service Reserve officers in Sec. 528 of the FSA of 1946 as amended, and is denied to AID Foreign Service Reserve officers in Sec. 603(b) of Executive Order No. 10973 as amended (November 3, 1961), regarding Administration of Foreign Assistance and Related Functions.

14. There has been a rising tide of dissatisfaction with this career service system. See, for example, Elizabeth A. Bean and Herbert J. Horowitz, "Is the Foreign Service Losing Its Best Young Officers?" *Foreign Service Journal*, February 1968; also, "Task

Force VII, Stimulation of Creativity," U.S. Department of State, *Diplomacy for the 70's*.

15. See, for example, Argyris, "Some Causes of Organizational Ineffectiveness."

16. "The Department of State relies heavily (as it has for many years) on the recruitment of young college graduates who are brought in as junior Foreign Service Officers. In recent years, junior officer appointments have accounted for about four-fifths of the total number of Foreign Service Officer appointments. The Agency for International Development has relied almost exclusively on recruitment of more mature persons with specialized training and experience brought in at the middle and higher grades" (*Personnel for the New Diplomacy*, p. 66).

17. Testimony of David Bell, U.S., Congress, Senate Committee on Appropriations, *Personnel Administration and Operations of the Agency for International Development*, Special Hearings Before the Committee on Appropriations, 88th Cong., 1st sess., 8 May 1963, p. 9.

18. For example, the Kennedy, Johnson, and Nixon administrations requested of the Congress that certain AID personnel be allowed to participate in the State Department's Foreign Service Retirement and Disability system. The requests were turned down by the Congress because "it did not wish to take an action that would confer permanent status on the Agency" (testimony of Lane Dwinell, Assistant Administrator for Administration, AID, U.S., Congress, House Committee on Foreign Affairs, *Foreign Assistance Act of 1969*, part 5, Hearings Before the Committee on Foreign Affairs, 91st Cong., 1st sess., 14 July 1969, p. 901).

19. The desire for such flexibility was expressed in the Presidential Task Force Report which formed the basis for the legislation creating AID. "Success of U.S. efforts in assisting countries to obtain maximum growth will depend largely upon the Agency's ability to maintain a professional staff with high standards of motivation and performance. To this end, the personnel system will provide maximum flexibility in obtaining the best personnel available whether within or without the Federal Service. . . . The development of a separate career personnel system for AID personnel is unnecessary and undesirable" (President's Task Force on Foreign Economic Assistance, *An Act for International Development: A Program for the Decade of Development, Fiscal Year 1962*, Summary Presentation, General Foreign Policy Series, no. 169 [Washington, D.C.: U.S. Department of State, 1961], p. 136).

20. Testimony of David Bell, in *Personnel Administration*, pp. 6, 23. This did not seem to mean that the limited status employee would be laid off automatically if tenure were not granted after a certain period. Rather, he was the most vulnerable when personnel reductions were being carried out.

21. Jacob J. Kaplan, *The Challenge of Foreign Aid: Policies, Problems, and Possibilities* (New York: Praeger, 1967), pp. 389-90.

22. Gordon Tullock, *The Politics of Bureaucracy* (Washington, D.C.: Public Affairs Press, 1965), p. 42.

23. To illustrate: "In its investigation of the mores, values, procedures and system of rewards in the [State] Department and the Foreign Service," a State Department study group reported, "the Task Force found that all of these acted as barriers to creativity. We found that the value system of the Service respected precedent and conformity to standards . . . and that this led to resistance to innovation. . . . The Foreign Service has traditionally prided itself on being a kind of elite corps. While this view has been of value in contributing to the high professional standards which the Service has maintained, it has also produced a tendency toward insularity. . . . Too many [supervisors] seek to discourage [creative initiatives], either because, imbued with the values of the Service, they view the unconventional as by definition unsound. . . . This tendency is aggravated by the exaggerated respect for rank which is tradition in the Service" (U.S., Department of State, "Task Force VII, Stimulation of Creativity" in *Diplomacy for the 70's*, pp. 293, 311).

24. *Personnel for the New Diplomacy*, p. 77.

25. *Ibid.*, p. 77.

26. Department of State, "Task Force VII, Stimulation of Creativity," in *Diplomacy for the 70's*, p. 324.

27. Carroll McKibbin, "Attrition of Foreign Service Officers: Then and Now," *Foreign Service Journal*, May 1969, as cited in Mosher, "Some Observations about Foreign Service Reforms," pp. 607-9.

28. The difference between AID and the Foreign Service was even apparent in the way the officers and offices of the two agencies looked. As John Harr described it, "The embassy proper is a distinctive institution and its ambience is likely to have traces of elegance. . . . Normally the atmosphere is sedate; officers are prone to wear vests and hardly anyone walks around in shirtsleeves. . . . AID will be in a different building . . . and the atmosphere usually will lack distinctiveness. It will be like the headquarters of any of a thousand business firms in the capital city, with local overtones such as faulty elevators and spartan furnishings. One is likely to see suntanned technicians, clad in sandals and khaki shorts, just in from a field project" (*The Professional Diplomat* [Princeton: Princeton University Press, 1969], pp. 298-99).

29. *Personnel for the New Diplomacy*, p. 25.

30. *Foreign Service Journal*, June 1965, p. 30.

31. *Toward a Modern Diplomacy: A Report to the American Foreign Service Association* (Washington, D.C.: American Foreign Service Association, 1968), p. 37.

32. U.S., Congress, House Committee on Foreign Affairs, *Foreign Assistance Act of 1969*, part 6, Hearings Before the Committee on Foreign Affairs, 91st Cong., 1st sess., 22 July 1969, p. 1193.

33. Kaplan, *Challenge of Foreign Aid*, p. 390. This higher rate, however, seems to have been a result not only of voluntary resignation but of significant personnel reductions as well. Without a further breakdown of the turnover figure into voluntary and forced separation, it is difficult to use it as evidence of resignation resulting from employee insecurity.

34. U.S., Congress, Senate Committee on Appropriations, *Personnel Administration and Operations of Agency for International Development*, Report of Senator Gale W. McGee to the Committee on Appropriations, 88th Cong., 1st sess., S. Doc. 57, 29 November 1963, p. 26.

35. Harvey S. Perloff, *Alliance for Progress: A Social Invention in the Making* (Baltimore: Johns Hopkins Press, 1969), pp. 149-50.

36. Peter M. Blau, *Bureaucracy in Modern Society* (New York: Random House, 1956), p. 64 of paperback edition.

37. *Personnel for the New Diplomacy*, p. 118. The report does recommend a career system for "those responsible for planning and managing overseas programs."

38. *Ibid.*, pp. 25-26. In the same vein, Senator McGee's report, cited above, states that "because of pressures from various sources numerous marginal employees were retained on the Agency's rolls. . . . The authority given in the Foreign Assistance Act of 1961, to initiate a 'selection out' process of marginal employees was begun only belatedly. . . . As this procedure affects only the FSR category of personnel, it leaves 2,600 civil service employees at the Washington level not subject to the selection out process and some means should be devised to rid the Agency of any deadwood in this category" (Senate Committee on Appropriations, Report of Sen. Gale W. McGee, p. 30).

39. It is interesting that the lawyers, rather than the economists, were the powerful and the innovating in an organization concerned with economic development. This occurred at the IBRD as well. "It was extraordinary," an IBRD official recounted, "how in the early days the legal department produced broad concepts and ideas and suggestions, and gradually management began to expect the lawyers to have these ideas rather than the economists" (quoted in Mason and Asher, *World Bank Since Bretton Woods*, p. 75).

40. The distinction I am making is similar to one made by Blau in describing employee attitudes toward change. "In the study of the federal agency, the attitudes of a group of officials toward changes in regulations, which occurred frequently, were ascertained and related to their competence as [welfare] investigators. Not one of the more competent half of this group, but most of all the less competent half, voiced objections to these recurrent innovations. From a purely rational standpoint, the opposite finding might have been expected: the agent most familiar with existing

regulations and most adept in applying them presumably should have been more disturbed when they were superseded by new ones" (*Bureaucracy in Modern Society*, pp. 90-91). See also Peter Blau, *The Dynamics of Bureacracy: A Study of Interpersonal Relations in Two Government Agencies*, rev. ed. (Chicago: University of Chicago Press, 1955), p. 245.

CHAPTER III: THE MISFIT

1. Michel Crozier points out that, in general, the need for adaptive behavior presents itself at the lower echelons of a bureacracy, because they are in closest contact with the public they serve and hence with the transformations occurring in society at large. But the inability to innovate that he describes results from almost exactly opposite reasons than the inability I discuss. Crozier says that "decisions must be made where power is located, i.e., on the top." Yet the top cannot be adaptive, he says, because of the "strata isolation" and concomitant lack of communication that is characteristic of bureacracy. Although the challenge to adapt also presents itself at the lower echelons in my foreign aid case, the inability to respond results not from a lack of power but, to the contrary, from an unusual degree of power vested in a lower echelon man who is incapable of exercising it responsively. See *Bureaucratic Phenomenon*, p. 195.

2. "When Government Works," *The Public Interest*, no. 18 (Winter 1970), pp. 42-43.

3. Testimony of David Bell, in *Personnel Administration*, pp. 13-14. My use of this passage here is not quite fair, since Bell was hedging against the criticism that the Washington staff was too large.

4. For example, John Harr comments on the same "lack of a systematic, meaningful dialogue between Washington and the field" in the case of the State Department and its embassies. "The feelings run worse from the field to Washington than vice versa. Operators in the field are prone to see Washington as a great bureaucratic sludge which is either unresponsive when something is wanted or bristling with bright ideas that no one needs" (*The Professional Diplomat*, pp. 301-2).

5. Milton Esman and John Montgomery, for example, state that the technical assistance in public administration of U.S. foreign aid programs is based on outmoded principles dating back to the 1930's. "For nearly a generation scholars of public administration in the United States have been reacting vigorously against the simplistic 'economy and efficiency' models of the 1930's. At least four influential schools of thought have emerged to reinvigorate the discipline. . . . But the perceptions have not yet been strongly felt in the U.S. foreign aid programs, where the concerns of the 1930's have remained dominant. . . . Little effort has been made in the aid programs to apply this knowledge [gained from the behavioral approach to public administration] to administration of development programs in cooperating countries. . . . AID itself has been aware of this interest [in the interdependence of administrative behavior and institutions with culture] and has sponsored important research in development administration, but the fruits of this research have not had a prominent place either in AID's operating doctrine or in its practices" ("Systems Approach to Technical Cooperation," pp. 513-14).

6. Louis Hartz, *The Founding of New Societies* (New York: Harcourt, Brace & World, 1964), pp. 3, 6.

7. William D. Rogers, *The Twilight Struggle: The Alliance for Progress and the Politics of Development in Latin America* (New York: Random House, 1967), pp. 223-24.

8. Hartz, *Founding of New Societies*, pp. 8-9. As outlined above, of course, the theory seems contradictory. One cannot be immobile *and* evolve at the same time. A "case study" by Samuel Huntington, however, shows that a more refined treatment of the subject can yield convincing results. Briefly, one can identify immobile and evolving *features* within the same society. In the American case, for example, Huntington argues that the political system is archaic, dating back to the time of colonization, while the social and institutional aspects of the country have evolved considerably under

their new-found freedom. See "Political Modernization: America vs. Europe," *World Politics* 18 (April 1966): 378-414.

9. See, for example, Everett E. Hagen, *On the Theory of Social Change* (Homewood, Ill.: The Dorsey Press, 1962), part 3.

10. Blau, *Dynamics of Bureaucracy*, pp. 112, 114, 115, 253, 263.

11. *Ibid.*, p. 112. Italics mine.

12. As reported in W. Wendell Blancké, *The Foreign Service of the United States* (New York: Praeger, 1969), pp. 236-37.

13. Testimony of James Fowler, Acting U.S. Coordinator, Alliance for Progress, AID, in U.S., Congress, House Committee on Foreign Affairs, *New Directions for the 1970's: Toward a Strategy of Inter-American Development*, Hearings Before the Subcommittee on Inter-American Affairs, 91st Cong., 1st sess., 25 February 1969, p. 595.

14. Department of State, "Task Force V, Personnel Perquisites: Nonsalary Compensations and Allowances," *Diplomacy for the 70's*, p. 153.

15. *Ibid.*, p. 1.

16. Indeed, the AID employee who was trying to make friends among the host country persons he met would often find the PX, liquor, and APO privileges to his disadvantage. The existence of PX products in his home would be noted by his foreign acquaintances as a sign of his lack of faith in the local market and the "easy life" abroad. He often found that what he had hoped were friendships were unpleasantly tinged by requests to obtain things at the PX. Thus, the PX "benefit" could actually be of negative value to the AID technician trying to make a go of it in his new culture.

17. To illustrate: "The alternative of 'living on the economy' was prohibitively expensive in many places . . . and the U.S. Government often found it cheaper and easier to build compounds and set up commissaries than to triple or quadruple living allowances. . . . Whereas a small, remote embassy may have managed to get along quite comfortably . . . once a big military assistance or AID mission arrives there must be virtually total logistic support. . . . In [AID] concentration countries, it is not unusual for the AID staff to outnumber embassy, service attachés, USIS, and Peace Corps headquarters staff combined" (Blancké, *Foreign Service of the United States*, pp. 122, 148).

18. Department of State, "Task Force V, Personnel Perquisites: Nonsalary Compensations and Allowances," *Diplomacy for the 70's*, p. 212. The group made twenty-one recommendations, all of which sought to extend the perquisites in existence. Among them: (2) The Standard Regulations should be revised to permit reimbursement of extraordinary subsistence expenses of the employee and all family members when the employee is required to occupy temporary quarters without adequate kitchen facilities. . . . (3) The home service transfer allowance should be increased to $12 per adult and $6 for each family member under 11 years of age. . . . (8) Legislative authority should be sought to provide for kindergarten educational allowances. . . . (11) That the present transfer allowance be divided into two categories, establishing a wardrobe allowance to cover extraordinary wardrobe expenses resulting from inter-zone transfers and a displacement allowance for reimbursement for those extraordinary expenses incident to all transfers with separate rate, payment, or reimbursement for each. . . . (12) The Standardized Regulations should be revised to reflect four climatic zones for clothing transfer allowance purposes . . . " (pp. 150-51).

19. I take the idea of "matches" and "mismatches" from Paul Lawrence and Jay W. Lorsch, *Developing Organizations: Diagnosis and Action* (Reading, Mass.: Addison-Wesley, 1969), pp. 27 ff.

20. "It cannot be said that the Bank has been an outstanding leader in applying new techniques of project appraisal or analysis of development processes. . . . The Bank has perhaps been less venturesome than some other project lenders, at least until recently, in exploring new avenues of investment. . . . Project lending by the Bank in some respects has been based on a narrower concept of the development process than has the project lending of either the Inter-American Development Bank or the U.S. Agency for International Development" (Mason and Asher, *World Bank Since Bretton Woods*, pp. 257-58).

CHAPTER IV: THE INSTITUTIONALIZATION OF OUTSIDE CRITICISM

1. For example: (1) At least 50 percent of the gross tonnage of AID-financed commodities must be shipped on U.S.-flag carriers (Merchant Marine Act of 1936 as amended); U.S.-flag shipping rates, especially for tramp shipping, are generally higher than those of other-country carriers; the provision also has the effect of limiting AID lending for projects involving high gross tonnage commodity exports. (2) Procurement was limited almost exclusively to U.S. sources, largely at Treasury Department insistence, which adds considerable costs to borrowers; the source of this authority is AID manual orders, and the loan approval procedure in which the Treasury has a veto (for the relaxing of these limitations since 1970, see chapter 6). (3) Assistance must be terminated not only when expropriation without adequate compensation occurs, but where there is an unpaid, uncontested debt to a private U.S. citizen in the recipient country (Section 620[c] and [e] of the Foreign Assistance Act). (4) No assistance can be provided for productive enterprises competitive with U.S. industry unless the country agrees to limit exports to the United States to 20 percent of assisted enterprise output (Section 620[d] of FAA). (5) Assistance is reduced if the country has seized and fined U.S. vessels in international waters and fails to pay any U.S. government claims for amounts expended in reimbursing owners under the Fisherman's Protective Act, Section 5. (6) Public Law 480 ("Food for Peace") limits recipient-country exports of similar, as well as the same, commodities as those imported under PL 480; e.g., if PL 480 wheat is imported, then recipient-country exports of corn or rice are prohibited or limited. See House Committee on Foreign Affairs, *Foreign Assistance Act of 1969*, part 6, pp. 1193-94.

2. For AID's publicity about U.S. equipment sales, and congressional rebukes for it, see U.S., Congress, Senate Committee on Foreign Relations, *Foreign Economic Assistance, 1973*, Hearings Before the Committee on Foreign Relations, 93d Cong., 1st sess., 26 June 1973, pp. 155-209.

3. "President Kennedy is reported to have complained repeatedly about the need to expend on foreign aid an unduly large proportion of his limited leverage with the Congress" (Kaplan, *Challenge of Foreign Aid*, p. 163).

4. Testimony of John Hannah, U.S., Congress, House Committee on Appropriations, *Foreign Assistance and Related Agencies, Appropriations for 1971*, part 2, Hearings Before the Subcommittee on Foreign Operations and Related Agencies, 91st Cong., 2d sess., 18 March 1970, p. 167.

The matter of U.S. foreign aid, its unpopularity, and the consequent constraints upon its action has been discussed in the terms outlined above in sources such as Richard Fenno, *The Power of the Purse: Appropriations Politics in Congress* (Boston: Little, Brown & Co., 1966); William L. Morrow, "Legislative Control of Administrative Discretion: The Case of Congress and Foreign Aid," *Journal of Politics* 30 (November 1968): 985-1011; David B. Truman, "The Domestic Politics of Foreign Aid," *Proceedings of the Academy of Political Science* 27 (January 1962): 62-72; Levinson and de Onis, *Alliance That Lost Its Way*; and Wall, *Charity of Nations*, chaps. 3 and 4.

5. The idea of freeing the foreign aid program from annual congressional appropriations has been proposed in one form or another for a long time, and predates the creation of AID under the Kennedy administration. In 1959, the Senate Foreign Relations Committee proposed a five-year development loan program to be financed by Treasury borrowing at the rate of $1 billion a year. The proposal was defeated. See Fenno, *Power of the Purse*, pp. 518-19.

6. And, as David Truman points out, the lack of professional consensus about matters in the field makes the subject conducive to easy sniping by laymen — in this case, the lay watchdogs. "Foreign aid . . . is a novel if not wholly unprecedented instrument of national policy, with all that such newness implies in controversy and uncertainty. It is at its heart technical in character, comparable in complexity to the problems of modern military strategy and weaponry. Unlike the military sector, however, its spokesmen lack the authority with which an established and respected professional corps can protect its jurisdiction from the vicissitudes of controversial novelty.

Especially when circumstances permit only slight consensus among the real experts, every man can be his own expert on foreign aid; he can challenge the specialist with a degree of impunity that he is unlikely to enjoy if he ventures into the realm of the military or even into that of diplomacy in its more conventional forms. . . . Where time and convention have not surrounded a technical policy and process with professional authority and with supporting myths and symbols, public discourse is peculiarly likely to be couched in a language whose simplifications are poorly adapted to the goals of the enterprise and to the effectiveness of the larger political system" ("The Domestic Politics of Foreign Aid," p. 146).

7. House Committee on Foreign Affairs, *Foreign Assistance Act of 1969*, part 6, p. 1193.

8. Anthony Downs relates the feedback question to the probability that a bureaucracy will become ossified. "If a major bureau becomes absolutely rigid in its behavior, its sovereign will soon begin hearing loud feedbacks from clients, suppliers, regulatees, rivals, and allies. Hence the bureau will find itself under strong pressure to become more flexible. The rigidity cycle is least likely to occur in bureaus that are under strong and constant pressure from such feedbacks. . . . Bureaus that serve the electorate directly are less likely to ossify than those that do not. Excessive rigidity in such bureaus as the State Department, AID, and the military services, therefore, may persist for extensive periods" (*Inside Bureaucracy*, pp. 163-64).

9. In February of 1965, voluntary restraints on direct U.S. foreign investment were introduced, whereby companies were asked to invest no more than a certain percentage of actual direct investment during a 1962-64 base period. In January of 1968 the controls were made mandatory and more restrictive.

10. This assumption has been disputed on the grounds that tied aid dollars may simply result in the substitution of these dollars for foreign exchange that would have been acquired anyway for purchase of goods in the United States in the absence of aid. That is, the amount of foreign exchange "released" by aid dollars may be used to import from third countries, according to this argument, thus resulting in as much of a net outflow of dollars as in the case of local-cost financing. Conversely, it is said, local-cost financing can generate new demand for U.S. exports if it is associated with a project using some U.S. equipment. The project will require future purchases of spare parts and replacements from the U.S.; and, less directly, by increasing national income, the project will increase correspondingly the demand for imports, including those from the U.S., by way of the function that relates import demand to GNP growth.

I am interested here in Treasury power over AID resulting from its responsibility to enforce certain policy directives. Whether or not tied aid can lead to additional imports from the U.S. has been discussed widely elsewhere. See, for example, Lachman, *The Local Currency Proceeds of Foreign Aid* (Paris: OECD, 1968), chapter 4; statement of William S. Gaud, Administrator, AID, in U.S., Congress, Joint Economic Committee, *A Review of Balance of Payments Policies*, Hearings Before the Subcommittee on International Exchange and Payments, 91st Cong., 1st sess., 13 January 1969, pp. 90-97.

11. Joint Economic Committee, *Review of Balance of Payments Policies*, p. 92. Other material in this paragraph of the text is a paraphrase of the same source. A comprehensive discussion of the intricacies of additionality procedures can be found in Organization of American States, *External Financing for Latin American Development* (Baltimore: Johns Hopkins Press, 1971), pp. 145-57.

12. Quoting, again, Administrator Gaud: "If AID credits are to be covered fully by additional U.S. exports, part of a host country's imports must be diverted from foreign sources of supply to the United States . . . through import and exchange controls. The United States has long viewed such controls as serious obstacles to efficient development. It has been a goal of AID to encourage removal of these controls to encourage free operation of market forces. Although systems of controls have not actually been established as a result of our efforts to obtain additionality, those efforts may serve as incentive to delay dismantling of existing systems.

"In several instances AID positive lists have been so limited that countries could not draw down available funds at a reasonable pace, and put them to use for development. Importers were simply reluctant to use AID funds to purchase goods subject to our procedures and at higher prices.

"Where AID, together with Treasury and Commerce, has been particularly concerned with additionality shortfalls in an individual country, we have frequently had to spend months negotiating an additionality agreement. This is a complex and sensitive subject, and has tended to divert attention from negotiations on self-help and other important development objectives. Both the United States and the host government spend too much time and energy talking about the wrong subjects" (Joint Economic Committee, *Review of Balance of Payments Policies*, p. 95).

13. Paul L. Montgomery, "U.S. Restrictions Curb Bolivian Aid," *New York Times*, February 6, 1969, p. 9.

14. This fact was not made public, but was intimated in a story in the *New York Times* on June 13, 1969. See Benjamin Welles, "Nixon Gives Warm Greeting to Colombian Leader," p. 5.

15. See the so-called CECLA Report of the Latin American Special Economic Coordinating Committee, which met at Viña del Mar, Chile, in May of 1969. The presentation of the report was recounted in the *New York Times* on June 15, 1969. Benjamin Welles, "Nixon Is Told the 'Time Has Come for Action,' " sec. 4, p. 4.

16. Cited in House Committee on Foreign Affairs, *Foreign Assistance Act of 1969*, part 5, p. 1107.

17. An excellent detailed account of such incursions, and the problems they created, is to be found in Levinson and de Onis, *Alliance That Lost Its Way.*

18. EMBRATEL is Empresa Brasileira de Telecomunicações, a government enterprise. The quoted material is from AID, Brazil Mission, "Memo on Brazil — IRR-EMBRATEL Inter-Urban Telecommunications Project," LA/CD [Latin America/Capital Development], February 2, 1967, pp. 3, 4, 9, as cited in a memo from Judith Tendler to John Kaufman on "IRR for EMBRATEL Inter-Urban Telecommunications Project," (typewritten), p. 1.

19. Indeed, it is a pity that the agency, like most government bureaucracies, throws away its old files so regularly, in a continuing and desperate counterattack on its penchant for committing everything to paper. There is much more to be learned about the agency's development experience from draft working documents at fairly low levels concerning a project's application for financing and later execution, than from the guarded, higher-level documents that are classified. The latter type of document, so prized by the scholarly researcher, is often least useful because it is written at a stage of decisionmaking when many of the interesting problems have been resolved and conflicting positions reconciled by the use of neutral words.

20. There was one exception: the congressional criticism that aid-recipient countries were increasingly and alarmingly associated with repressive military governments. This concern resulted in Title IX of the Foreign Assistance Act of 1966, which required that the agency place emphasis "on assuring maximum participation in the task of economic development on the part of the people of the developing countries, through the encouragement to democratic private and local governmental institutions." This directive seemed rather naive in assuming that AID could curb the flood of military governments by financing "political development projects," and in pointing the finger of blame and putting the burden of change on the arm of American involvement that was least responsible for the fact that American foreign policy in Latin America was associated with military governments. Finally, this legislative directive to AID to get involved in the labor unions, the state legislatures, the peasant leagues, and the municipal administrations of the recipient countries could only be looked upon by the latter as a very intrusive step.

21. Blau also refers to the effects on an organization of a hostile environment, citing the labor unions and socialist parties of Imperial Germany as studied by Michels. "It was the efforts of their officials to protect their survival in a hostile environment that led to a preoccupation with strengthening the administrative apparatus and to a retreat from the original radical objectives to more moderate reform goals. . . . An interest in maintaining the organization promotes the displacement of goals if the original mis-

sion evokes intense hostility that endangers the organization's existence" (*Dynamics of Bureaucracy*, p. 248). See also *Bureaucracy in Modern Society*, pp. 95-96.

22. Indeed, the atrophy of human communication was felt by a young State Department Foreign Service Officer to be alleviated somewhat only by the fact that he was stationed in a hostile country, where it was not improper to exercise one's critical powers in talking about the host country. "Sometimes I think that one of the advantages of working in my area is that the foreign country is not considered friendly to the U.S. and therefore it is more acceptable to be more open and critical" (Argyris, "Some Causes of Organizational Ineffectiveness," p. 38).

23. "The [Foreign] Service has prized drafting ability above almost all other skills. We emphasize this skill in recruitment and reward it generously in our promotion system. The prize jobs in the Service are the reporting jobs. Foreign Service Inspectors habitually examine reporting officers' 'chron' files in order to determine whether there has been an adequate volume of production" (Department of State, "Task Force VII, Stimulation of Creativity, *Diplomacy for the 70's*, p. 314).

24. For example, "Writing has become an occupational disease of our service. . . . Little wonder that our ablest and most energetic officers literally seek out opportunities to report, whether the need is urgent or not" (*ibid.*).

CHAPTER V: THE ABUNDANCE OF DEVELOPMENT ASSISTANCE

1. See, for example, *Partners in Development* (The Pearson Report), pp. 78, 177; Mikesell, *Economics of Foreign Aid*, p. 141; Jagdish Bhagwati, "The Tying of Aid," in *Foreign Aid*, ed. Jagdish Bhagwati and Richard S. Eckaus (Baltimore: Penguin Books, 1970), pp. 235-93.

2. The role of the organizational factor in causing large projects has been referred to only infrequently and briefly, usually in the process of advocating the favorability of program lending over project lending. See Hollis B. Chenery, "Foreign Assistance and Economic Development," in *Capital Movements and Economic Development*, ed. John H. Adler (New York: St. Martin's Press, 1967), p. 280.

3. Chenery says that the project system of aid administration "contains perverse incentives in both donors and recipients to select large projects with a high import content *in order to minimize administrative effort and maximize the aid received*. . . . It is very doubtful that anything approaching the volume of resources transferred [under AID program assistance] could have taken place under present project procedures" (*ibid.*, pp. 280, 286). Italics mine.

An AID official stated the same position bluntly in testimony before Congress. The program loan mechanism was preferable to project assistance, he said, because the former was "the way to provide substantial assistance to a country, assistance that can mean a lot because it is *disbursed rapidly in a short period of time and in large volume*" (testimony of William T. Dentzer, in House Committee on Foreign Affairs, *New Directions for the 1970's*, p. 48). Italics mine.

4. There is considerable discussion of the project vs. program lending question in the literature. See H. W. Singer, "External Aid: For Plans or Projects?" *The Economic Journal* 75 (September 1965): 539-45; Albert O. Hirschman and Richard M. Bird, "Foreign Aid — A Critique and a Proposal," *Essays in International Finance*, no. 69 (New Jersey: International Finance Section, Department of Economics, Princeton University, July 1968); Arnold Harberger, "Issues Concerning Capital Assistance to Less Developed Countries: Comment," *Economic Development and Cultural Change* 22 (January 1974): 336-44.

5. The growth of the system had lagged behind the growth of demand. As is frequently the case in developing countries, there was some difficulty in making reliable forecasts of the system's future needs, since past growth records would not include the unattended demand which would surely surface when new facilities were added to the system.

6. AID, Brazil Mission, "Passo Real Hydroelectric Project," memo from Judith Tendler, Office of Development Planning (DPEC), to John Kaufmann (Assistant Director Development Planning), September 18, 1967, p. 1.

7. AID, Brazil Mission, "Memorandum of Conversation," William Wheeler, Office of Capital Development, August 3, 1967, as cited in AID, Brazil Mission, "Passo Real," memo from Judith Tendler to William Wheeler, April 11, 1968, p. 2.

8. Between 1963 and 1968, AID made twelve loans to Brazil for power — including funds for distribution, transmission, and power plant expansion as well as for the construction of hydro and thermal plants. The loans ranged from $5 million to $41 million, with more than half of them (7) being above $13 million (House Committee on Foreign Affairs, *New Directions for the 1970's*, p. 601).

9. Tendler, "Passo Real Hydroelectric Project," p. 1.

10. The rest of the imported items were for other equipment for the power plant, transmission lines, and distribution system ($5,861,000), for engineering ($1,500,000), for contingencies ($2,036,000), and for construction equipment ($5,550,000), which the power company would buy and lease to the local contractor. The last item was added to the import list some time after the original discussions about the loan — raising it to $24 million — and is dealt with in the third example below. The generators, at this point of the discussions, had already been taken off the import list. I use these particular cost estimates, even though they were superseded by more recent ones, because this was the only point at which an estimate was made of the items to be imported which could be produced locally. (From a Preliminary Estimate by ENRO [Office of Engineering], under the subheading "Items on Import List which are produced in Brazil," Attachment to "Passo Real," memo from Judith Tendler to John Kaufman, May 6, 1968.)

11. The mission made a point of not engaging in these negotiations between borrower and association and at most would send a representative for the purpose of clarifying any questions of AID lending procedure that might be raised.

Like most developing countries, Brazil has legislation seeking to protect its local producers. For goods which can be produced in the country, the Brazilian "Law of Similars" denies to foreign-financed or government projects the privileges such projects normally have to import goods free of substantial tariffs and taxes. The administrative entity which decides whether "similars" exist (CACEX in the Central Bank), and whether the imported product qualifies for waiving of import tariffs and taxes, usually consults with the association representing the local industry involved — in this case, ABDIB. The opinion of the industrial association is generally accepted as the basis for CACEX judgment. Needless to say, decisions about what can and cannot be produced locally involve a considerable amount of latitude, especially since the law allows "similars" to be imported if the local product cannot be delivered in accordance with the time schedule of the project. Hence the CACEX decision is often the result of bargaining between local firms and the government or borrowing entity; or the borrower changes the specifications slightly so as to make the product he desires to import "dissimilar" (the borrowing entity sometimes gets around the local firm or industry by promising it orders on a different project); or the decision is influenced by persuasion backed by financial or political influence. This consultative procedure, of course, encourages flamboyant claims on the part of local producers about what they can produce and when, derogatory comments about the local product by the government entity seeking foreign financing, allegations by local producers of discrimination against them by foreign assistance programs, and a generally heated atmosphere in which technical decisions must be made.

12. The story of these decisions is based on my own participation in many of them, my attendance at one of the meetings of negotiation between the manufacturers' association and the power company (which I related in the previously cited memo, "Passo Real," of May 6), and other unclassified memoranda concerning the subject in the files of the Office of Capital Development of the Brazil Mission.

13. Chap. 5 provides another example of AID-borrower-local industry bargaining over what could be imported. The IBRD and IDB also resorted during this period to some such form of discussion with Brazilian manufacturers' associations, to determine the size of the imported component of the projects they had financed.

14. Tendler, "Passo Real Hydroelectric Project," p. 1. (Italics mine.) This is a re-

counting of discussions that occurred when an AID team, of which I was a member, met with the company for a week at its headquarters during August of 1967.

15. This contrasts with the common explanation of organizational behavior in conflict with policy goals, according to which the individual's behavior is explained as the rational pursuit of a set of goals that is completely different, and related to his attempts to find security and/or advancement within his organization. See Blau, *Bureaucracy in Modern Society*, pp. 86-91.

16. AID, Brazil — Southern States Highway Maintenance Equipment, Proposal and Recommendations for the Review of the Development Loan Committee, AID-DLC/P-592, 1967. The material in this chapter is taken from pp. 8-9, 19-20 of this paper.

17. AID, Brazil Mission, Division of Highways, "Monthly Progress Report," January 1968, p. 3.

18. Indeed, this is what ultimately happened for one of the southern states, Rio Grande do Sul. The dollar value of the AID financing was more than halved in 1970 (from $13.3 million to $5.5 million) "due to an increase in Brazilian-made equipment to be provided for the project" (House Committee on Appropriations, *Foreign Assistance and Related Agencies, Appropriations for 1974*, part 2, p. 978).

19. Draft letter to the Sindicato, AID, Brazil Mission, Office of Capital Development, March 20, 1968, p. 1.

20. AID, Brazil Mission, airgram from Rio de Janeiro to AID Washington, "Monthly Status Dollar Capital Projects (December 1967 and January 1968)," January 31, 1968, p. 2.

21. Chap. 4 treats the phenomenon of borrower-country criticism which does not return to the aid entity in a useful form, and the resulting absence of constructive beneficiary feedback.

22. The literature of economic development has come upon other aid-financed project decisions that neglected better alternatives for similar reasons. See, for example, John W. Thomas, "The Choice of Technology in Developing Countries: The Case of Irrigation Tubewells in Bangladesh," n.d.; Robert Repetto, "Economic Aspects of Irrigation Project Design in East Pakistan," in *Development Policy II — The Pakistan Experience*, ed. Walter P. Falcon and Gustav F. Papanek (Cambridge: Harvard University Press, 1971); Carl H. Gotsch, "Tractor Mechanisation and Rural Development in Pakistan," *International Labour Review* 107 (February 1973): 133-66.

CHAPTER VI: FINANCING IMPORTS

1. This figure refers to fiscal year 1974. House Committee on Appropriations, *Foreign Assistance and Related Agencies, Appropriations for 1975*, part 2, p. 267.

2. IBRD figures for 1961-68 are from Mason and Asher, *World Bank Since Bretton Woods*, p. 278; IDB figures for 1969, from Dell, *Inter-American Development Bank*, p. 105. The IDB policy with respect to local cost financing is somewhat complicated; for a comprehensive discussion, see Dell, pp. 97-109.

3. In 1969, the United States allowed foreign exchange procurement with AID loans in all Latin American countries and in 1970 extended this modification to most less-developed countries. The resulting increase in aid-financed Third World procurement was not great, amounting to $34.9 million between late 1969 and mid-1973, about 7% of total AID-financed procurement during that period. The more significant untying, in terms of price competition, would be to the other developed countries — procedures already followed by most multilateral institutions. In 1970, the United States announced readiness to work with other aid donors to negotiate a reciprocal untying. These talks were suspended in 1971, at U.S. request, pending resolution of international monetary problems.

4. See, e.g., Alexis E. Lachman, *The Local Currency Proceeds of Foreign Aid* (Paris: OECD, 1968), chap. 3. The OECD's *Development Cooperation Review* for 1973 also has a good discussion of the bias against local cost financing, pp. 62-65.

5. For example, the IBRD justified its import-cost policy by saying that it was "a practical way of assuring that [the recipients] will mobilize their own resources to meet

a substantial part of the cost of the projects or programs concerned" (*The World Bank, IFC and IDA: Policies and Operations* [Washington, D.C., 1962], p. 38).

6. The two obvious alternatives are (1) to finance a certain percentage of a project without discriminating between foreign exchange and local costs, or (2) to provide financing in the form of general budgetary support. The alternatives, and the current system, are discussed widely in the literature cited at the beginning of this volume, as well as in the Lachman book cited above.

"Self help" also refers to non-project-related measures taken by a country to increase domestic savings and make improvements in other areas of monetary and fiscal policy.

7. See, for example, Howard Pack, "Employment and Productivity in Kenyan Manufacturing," Institute for Development Studies, University of Nairobi, August 1972; Louis T. Wells, Jr., "Economic Man and Engineering Man: Choice of Technology in a Low Wage Country," Economic Development Report no. 226, Harvard University Center for International Affairs, November 1972; James Pickett, D. J. C. Forsyth, and N. S. McBain, "The Choice of Technology, Economic Efficiency, and Employment in Developing Countries," Glasgow, February 1973; John E. Todd, "Size of Firm and Efficiency in Colombian Manufacturing," Research Memorandum no. 41, Williams College Center for Development Economics, October 1971; Albert Berry, "Relevance and Prospects of Small-Scale Industry in Colombia," Yale University Economic Growth Center Discussion Paper no. 142, April 1972.

8. See Thomas, "Choice of Technology in Developing Countries"; Gotsch, "Tractor Mechanisation and Rural Development in Pakistan"; Peter C. Timmer, "Choice of Technique in Indonesia," Food Research Institute Discussion Paper no. 72-4, 1972.

9. IBRD, *Transportation*, Sector Working Paper, January 1972, p. 27.

10. *Ibid*.

11. It may be that the rationale is used less because it makes sense than because it provides a seemingly good excuse for avoiding the administrative headaches of doing things a different way.

12. This point is also suggested by Hollis B. Chenery in "Trade, Aid and Economic Development," in *International Development, 1965*, ed. S. H. Robock and L. M. Soloman (Dobbs Ferry, N.Y.: Oceana Publications, 1966), p. 187, and in K. B. Griffin and J. L. Enos, "Foreign Assistance: Objectives and Consequences," *Economic Development and Cultural Change* 18 (April 1970):313-27. The authors claim to find an inverse relation between gross domestic savings as a percent of GDP and foreign savings as a percent of GDP. Papanek argues that, although this inverse correlation exists, it does not imply causality between aid and decreased saving; both variables, he says, are probably being determined by the economic and/or political situation. See Gustav F. Papanek, "The Effect of Aid and Other Resource Transfers on Savings and Growth in Less Developed Countries," *Economic Journal*, no. 327 (September 1972), pp. 934-50.

13. A similar argument has been made with respect to the effect of assistance availability at an aggregate level. The donor world posits a "foreign exchange gap" as a constant, from which it determines a desired level of foreign assistance. The availability of foreign assistance based on this concept of foreign exchange scarcity as a constant rather than a variable is said to make recipient governments feel less need to worry about financing imports with exports, raising domestic revenues, and providing for a domestic capital market. See Jacob P. Meerman, "Issues Concerning Capital Assistance to Less Developed Countries: Comment," *Economic Development and Cultural Change* 22 (January 1974): 338-40; Ronald I. McKinnon, *Money and Capital in Economic Development* (Washington, D.C.: The Brookings Institution, 1973), pp. 170-72.

14. This perception is not very far from the truth. Kaplan comments about the period during which he was involved in aid programs. Because the supply of projects was limited, he says, and because of the detailed engineering, market, and cost analyses required for an application for financing, "most engineering proposals that had been prepared in adequate detail had little difficulty in finding financing" (*The Challenge of Foreign Aid*, p. 55).

15. The two types of credit are interchangeable, of course, in the overlapping area of

items which could be procured locally or purchased abroad without the resistance of local protective interest groups and legislation. As shown in the above examples, however, the local veto of imports for aid-financed projects can often be persuaded away, or circumvented by the borrower's requiring specifications which are not customarily found in the local product. In the nonoverlapping area — products made exclusively abroad, local production that is clearly adequate, or products for which faraway purchase is never feasible (labor, electricity, etc.) — foreign and domestic credit can still be interchanged to the extent that one can alter the design of the project to reduce the share of local expenditures. Foreign and domestic credit are complements only in the nonreducible area of nonoverlapping items.

16. Kaplan suggests specifically that maintenance and operating expenditures were neglected "in the effort to find matching local currencies for aid projects," since these expenditures "could not be organized in the form of projects with large, direct foreign exchange costs" (*Challenge of Foreign Aid*, p. 292).

17. After writing this section, I found a remarkably similar discussion of this subject with respect to decisionmaking about aid-financed irrigation projects in Pakistan. "Left largely to their own devices in project design, the technical agencies [my project-makers] respond to the real forces apparent to them. . . . Within each agency, there are drives toward greater employment, prestige, and bounty that are inducement to propose more and bigger projects. . . . Although at the center [my policymakers] development funds may appear very sharply limited, to the agency the supply seems quite elastic at the actual cost of capital to them. At the center, the need to reduce capital-output and capital-labor ratios may be obvious, but to the agency it seems safest to adhere to conventional designs and conventional engineering practice, although these conventions probably developed in labor-scarce and capital-abundant economies" (Repetto, "Economic Aspects of Irrigation Project Design," p. 156).

CHAPTER VII:
THE ORGANIZATIONAL ECONOMY OF LARGE PROJECTS

1. See the considerable concern expressed and attention devoted to such estimates in the works cited in the introductory chapter of this volume.

2. Mason and Asher, *World Bank Since Bretton Woods*, p. 308. The quotation is from Warren C. Baum, "The Project Cycle," *Finance and Development* 7 (June 1970): 6.

3. This point is elaborated further in the conclusion.

4. Charles Blankstein, an AID official in Latin America and Washington, suggested an additional reason for money moving behavior. " 'Moving money,' " he wrote, "is not only important for bureaucratic reasons. It gives you credibility and clout with the local government" (Blankstein to Tendler, May 1972).

5. One is reminded here of the studies of Soviet managers of state-owned industry, who "find themselves under strain — pressured from above by political directives, production targets, and the promise of premiums if they meet these targets; but at the same time beleaguered by bottlenecks in the distribution of raw materials and other supplies" (Neil J. Smelser, *The Sociology of Economic Life* [Englewood Cliffs, N.J.: Prentice-Hall, 1963], pp. 83-84). One of the responses of these managers to the difficult production targets they face is to engage in "subquality production to reach the target level of output." The foreign assistance manager, likewise, engages in "subquality decisionmaking" in order to meet the same type of target, which, though not formally expressed, is implicit in the organizational world in which he must perform.

6. See, e.g., Downs, *Inside Bureaucracy*, p. 200; Charles Russell Fisher, "Spring Spending Spree," in *Inside the System*, ed. Charles Peters and Timothy J. Adams (New York: Praeger, 1970), pp. 280-83.

7. The proposed foreign assistance legislation for 1962 asked for "no-year" appropriations for development lending, to replace existing procedures which required that funds unspent by the end of the fiscal year be returned to the Treasury. The request was made because of "the relaxation of standards [that occurred] for approving aid projects toward the end of any fiscal year" (President's Task Force on Foreign Economic

Assistance, *An Act for International Development: A Program for the Decade of Development, Fiscal Year 1962*, p. ix). It is ironic that, as can be seen from any set of congressional hearings on foreign assistance appropriations, the new no-year appropriations did not change the pressures that caused a "relaxation of standards" very much. Congress pointed to unexpended balances as proof that the foreign assistance agency did not need as much as it was asking for.

8. In the same vein, Kaplan writes that the fact that IBRD loans to Mexico and Venezuela increased remarkably after the IDB came into being "suggested to some a desire to capture from a new competitor the best available projects in the two Latin American countries whose debt service prospects are strongest" (*Challenge of Foreign Aid*, p. 363).

The Jackson Report comments on the occurrence of the same type of competition between the agencies of the United Nations Development Program, which deals largely with technical assistance. " 'What exists today is inter-Agency rivalry for projects, each Agency insisting, almost as a matter of right, to get a slice of the country pie, regardless of the value and propriety of the project from the country's point of view, at its particular stage of development.' The views of the Resident Representatives were eloquently summed up in the heartfelt cry of one of them: 'Get the salesmen out of the system!' " (vol. 2, p. 76). The passage cited in the quote is from the report of a U.N. Resident Representative.

9. IBRD, Statement to the Board of Governors, September 3, 1968, as cited in *A Study of the Capacity of the United Nations Development System* (The Jackson Report), vol. 1, p. 19; IDB, *Proceedings*, Tenth Meeting of the Board of Governors, Guatemala, April 1969, p. 70.

10. Owens and Shaw, *Development Reconsidered*, p. 152.

11. Mikesell, for example, writes that although the flow of project assistance may be irregular, "this is a matter of aid technique which might be dealt with by an improvement in the project-financing process. Much more fundamental is the principle that the *level* of aid should be determined by gap calculations based on growth models, rather than directly related to the ability of a country to formulate a stream of aid-worthy projects" (*Economics of Foreign Aid*, p. 170).

12. At the same time that outcries were being heard over the cutbacks in congressional appropriations for foreign aid at the turn of the decade, the country mission in one of the large aid-recipient countries was desperately working, along with the help of the Washington headquarters, to get together a group of projects large enough to absorb the funds available, even though those funds were substantially less than in previous years.

13. See, for example, Chenery and Strout, "Foreign Assistance and Economic Development," *American Economic Review* 56 (September 1966): 679-733; John C. H. Fei and Douglas S. Paauw, "Foreign Assistance and Self-Help: A Reappraisal of Development Finance," *Review of Economics and Statistics* 67 (August 1965): 251-67; Ronald I. McKinnon, "Foreign Exchange Constraints in Economic Development and Efficient Aid Allocation," *Economic Journal* 74 (June 1965): 388-409; P. N. Rosenstein-Rodan, "International Aid for Underdeveloped Countries," *The Review of Economics and Statistics* 43 (May 1961): 107-38; Alan M. Strout and Paul S. Clark, "Aid, Performance, Self-Help and Need," AID Discussion Paper no. 20, July 1969.

14. See the series *World Bank Staff Occasional Papers*, distributed by the Johns Hopkins University Press, Baltimore, Md.

15. Repetto, "Economic Aspects of Irrigation Project Design," p. 157.

16. Robert L. Peabody and Francis E. Rourke point out that rules requiring bureaucratic secrecy have been shown to be subject to extensive evasion. "The device of leaking information to the public serves many purposes, not least important of which, perhaps, is the fact that it provides a technique for arousing public support for policies that may have been rejected within the privacy of executive deliberations" ("Public Bureaucracies," in *Handbook of Organizations*, ed. James G. March [Chicago: Rand McNally, 1965], p. 825.

17. Or, as Thomas Schelling says in discussing the role of systems analysis and

PPBS in government, "[Such techniques] require a consumer, some responsible person or body that wants an orderly technique for bringing judgment to bear on a decision" ("PPBS and Foreign Affairs," in U.S., Congress, Senate Committee on Government Operations, *Planning-Programming-Budgeting*, Inquiry of the Subcommittee on National Security and International Operations for the Committee on Government Operations [Washington, D.C.: GPO, 1970], p. 111).

18. Repetto, "Economic Aspects of Irrigation Project Design," p. 155.

19. "Work expands so as to fill the time available for its completion" (C. Northcote Parkinson, *Parkinson's Law and Other Studies in Administration* [Boston: Houghton Mifflin, 1957], p. 20). Or, as Harry Johnson says, "There is some danger that the emerging popularity of 'cost-benefit analysis' will lead to more and more scarce resources being devoted to the allocation of funds among projects and less and less being available for the projects themselves. It is a well-known characteristic of bureaucracies that, the less money they have to spend, the more time and effort they devote to deciding exactly how to spend it" (Harry G. Johnson, "The 'Crisis of Aid' and The Pearson Report." A lecture delivered at the University of Edinburgh on 6 iii 1970. [Edinburgh: At the University Press, 1970], p. 219).

20. The IBRD, the development assistance institution considered most rigorous in its project evaluation technique, "is still reproached for . . . its sometimes slow and cumbersome process of project analysis and loan decision" (*Partners in Development* [The Pearson Report]).

21. For good descriptions of this problem, see Albert O. Hirschman and Richard M. Bird, "Foreign Aid — A Critique and a Proposal," and Meerman, "Issues Concerning Capital Assistance to Less Developed Countries: Comment." See further discussion of this point in the concluding chapter.

22. Hirschman and Bird, "Foreign Aid — A Critique and a Proposal."

23. Mason and Asher, *World Bank Since Bretton Woods*, p. 237.

24. McKinnon, *Money and Capital in Economic Development*, pp. 176-77.

25. *Ibid*. It has been proposed elsewhere, though not with the same justification, that foreign assistance should be used to finance the guarantee of securities issued by recipient countries in the international capital market. See Clark, *American Aid for Development*, p. 182.

26. The McKinnon book, it should be noted, does not purport to be a study of foreign assistance; it is an analysis of the subject of financial underdevelopment.

27. "Dissatisfied with what they consider to be the slow rate of development of Bank lending, [certain economists in the Bank] were extolling the merits of 'impact loans' and urging more local expenditure financing" (Mason and Asher, *World Bank Since Bretton Woods*, p. 275).

28. C. Peter Timmer provides a good example from Indonesia of the inability of an AID-financed consultant team to design a highway in keeping with the relative scarcity of capital and abundance of labor in that country. ("Choice of Technique in Indonesia," p. 14.) Mason and Asher state that although the technical departments of the IBRD were for a long time aware of the advisability of using labor in road construction projects, there was nevertheless "no very persistent pressure to bring this about." At the urging of the directors, a report on labor-equipment substitution in road construction was issued in 1965, which was "rather perfunctory and inconclusive." Since 1970, the IBRD has been sponsoring research in this area. (*World Bank Since Bretton Woods*, p. 244, n. 22.)

29. See material cited in chapter 6, nn. 7 and 8.

Chapter VIII: Conclusion

1. The discussion in this paragraph of environmental uncertainty and vertical integration is based on Thompson's *Organizations in Action*, chaps. 3, 4, and 5, and Lawrence and Lorsch's *Organization and Environment*, chaps. 1 and 8.

2. Thompson, *Organizations in Action*, p. 41.

3. Mason and Asher, *World Bank Since Bretton Woods*, p. 334.

4. K. W. Taylor, "The Pre-Investment Function in the International Development System," *International Development Review* 12 (1970): 4, as cited in Mason, p. 313. The Jackson Report on the UNDP evaluated this change in the IBRD in terms of poaching by the IBRD on UNDP territory. "While the extension of UN Services toward the provision of capital [in addition to technical assistance] has been checked. . . . the extension of the IBRD's services both to pre-investment and some forms of technical assistance has been considerable. . . . This is an enlargement of the IBRD's approach and . . . although UNDP was established to meet such specific needs, and can do so over a broader field, it has, in fact, been unable to meet all demands. . . . It remains true that a more rational distribution of resources would be obtained if multilateral technical assistance and pre-investment work were channeled through the body set up for that purpose" (vol. 2, pp. 17-18).

5. John H. Adler, "The World Bank's Concept of Development — An In-House *Dogmengeschichte*," in *Development and Planning: Essays in Honour of Paul Rosenstein-Rodan*, ed. Jagdish N. Bhagwati and Richard S. Eckaus (Cambridge, Mass.: M.I.T. Press, 1973), p. 39.

6. IBRD, "Substitution of Labor for Equipment in Road Construction," Projects Department, Report no. TO-477 (May 1965).

7. IBRD, *Transportation*, Sector Working Paper, January 1972.

8. Adler, "The World Bank's Concept of Development."

9. Bruce F. Johnston and Peter Kilby, *Agriculture and Structural Transformation: Economic Strategies in Late Developing Countries* (London: Oxford University Press, 1975), forthcoming.

10. Richard Patten, Belinda Dapice, and Walter Falcon, "An Experiment in Rural-Employment Creation: Indonesia's Kabupaten Development Program," n.d., p. 13.

11. John W. Mellor and Uma J. Lele, "Growth Linkages of the New Foodgrain Technologies," *Indian Journal of Agricultural Economics* (January-March 1973), p. 43.

12. Carl H. Gotsch, "Economics, Institutions and Employment Generation in Rural Areas" (xeroxed), Harvard University, August 1973.

13. Walter P. Falcon, "Agricultural Employment in Less Developed Countries: General Situation, Research Approaches, and Policy Palliatives," IBRD Economic Staff (Consultant) Working Paper no. 113, April 1971.

14. Deryke Belshaw and Robert Chambers, "A Management Systems Approach to Rural Development," Discussion Paper no. 161, Institute for Development Studies, University of Nairobi, January 1973.

BIBLIOGRAPHY

Adler, John H. "The World Bank's Concept of Development — An In-House *Dogmengeschichte.*" In *Development and Planning: Essays in Honour of Paul Rosenstein-Rodan*, edited by Jagdish N. Bhagwati and Richard S. Eckhaus. Cambridge: M.I.T. Press, 1973.

Argyris, Chris. "Some Causes of Organizational Ineffectiveness Within the Department of State." Occasional Paper no. 2, Center for International Systems Research. Washington, D.C.: Department of State, 1966.

Asher, Robert E. *Development Assistance in the Seventies: Alternatives for the United States.* Washington, D.C.: The Brookings Institution, 1970.

Bean, Elizabeth A., and Horowitz, Herbert J. "Is the Foreign Service Losing Its Best Young Officers?" *Foreign Service Journal*, February 1968.

Belshaw, Deryke, and Chambers, Robert. "A Management Systems Approach to Rural Development." Discussion Paper no. 161, Institute for Development Studies, University of Nairobi. January 1973.

Berry, R. Albert. "The Relevance and Prospects of Small Scale Industry in Colombia." Center Discussion Paper no. 142, Yale University Economic Growth Center. April 1972.

Bhagwati, Jagdish. "The Tying of Aid." In *Foreign Aid*, edited by Jagdish Bhagwati and Richard S. Eckhaus. Baltimore: Penguin Books, 1970.

Blancké, W. Wendell. *The Foreign Service of the United States.* New York: Praeger, 1969.

Blau, Peter M. *Bureaucracy in Modern Society.* New York: Random House, 1969. Paperback ed.

———. *The Dynamics of Bureaucracy: A Study of Interpersonal Relations in Two Government Agencies.* 2d rev. ed. Chicago: University of Chicago Press, 1963.

Burns, Tom, and Stalker, G. M. *The Management of Innovation.* London: Tavistock Publications, 1961.

Chenery, Hollis B. "Foreign Assistance and Economic Development." In *Capital Movements and Economic Development*, edited by John H. Adler. New York: St. Martin's Press, 1967.

———. "Trade, Aid and Economic Development." In *International Development, 1965*, edited by S. H. Robock and L. M. Soloman. New York: St. Martin's Press, 1967.

———, and Strout, Alan. "Foreign Assistance and Economic Development," *American Economic Review* 56 (September 1966): 679-733.

Clark, Paul G. *American Aid for Development.* New York: Praeger, 1972.

Commission on International Development. *Partners in Development* (The Pearson Report). Report of the Commission on International Development. New York: Praeger, 1969.

Committee on Foreign Affairs Personnel. *Personnel for the New Diplomacy* (The Herter Report). Report of the Committee on Foreign Affairs Personnel. Washington, D.C.: Carnegie Endowment for International Peace, 1962.

Crozier, Michel. *The Bureaucratic Phenomenon.* Chicago: University of Chicago Press, Phoenix Books, 1967.

Dell, Sidney. *The Inter-American Development Bank: A Study in Development Financing.* New York: Praeger, 1972.

Dill, William R. "Environment as an Influence on Managerial Autonomy." *Administrative Science Quarterly* 2 (March 1958): 409-43.

Downs, Anthony. *Inside Bureaucracy.* Boston: Little, Brown & Co., 1966.

Eicher, Carl; Zalla, Thomas; Kocher, James; and Winch, Fred. "Employment Generation in African Agriculture." Research Report no. 9, Institute of International Agriculture, Michigan State University. July 1970.

Esman, Milton J., and Montgomery, John D. "Systems Approach to Technical Cooperation." *Public Administration Review* 29 (September-October 1969): 507-39.

Falcon, Walter P. "Agriculture Employment in Less Developed Countries: General Situation, Research Approaches, and Policy Palliatives." IBRD Economic Staff (Consultant) Working Paper no. 113. April 1971.

Fei, John C. H., and Paauw, Douglas S. "Foreign Assistance and Self-Help: A Reappraisal of Development Finance." *Review of Economics and Statistics* 67 (August 1965): 251-67.

Fenno, Richard F., Jr. *The Power of the Purse: Appropriations Politics in Congress.* Boston: Little, Brown & Co., 1966.

Fisher, Charles Russell. "Spring Spending Spree." In *Inside the System,* edited by Charles Peters and Timothy J. Adams. New York: Praeger, 1970.

Foster, George C. *Traditional Cultures and the Impact of Technological Change.* New York: Harper & Row, 1962.

Gotsch, Carl H. "Economics, Institutions and Employment Generation in Rural Areas." Harvard University. August 1973.

———. "Tractor Mechanisation and Rural Development in Pakistan." *International Labour Review* 107 (February 1973): 113-60.

Griffin, K. B., and Enos, J. L. "Foreign Assistance: Objectives and Consequences." *Economic Development and Cultural Change* 18 (April 1970), pp. 313-27.

Hagen, Everett E. *On the Theory of Social Change.* Homewood, Illinois: The Dorsey Press, 1962.

Harberger, Arnold. "Issues Concerning Capital Assistance to Less Developed Countries." *Economic Development and Cultural Change* 20 (July 1972): 631-40.

Harr, John E. *The Professional Diplomat.* Princeton: Princeton University Press, 1969.

Hartz, Louis. *The Founding of New Societies.* New York: Harcourt, Brace & World, 1964.

Hayter, Teresa. *Aid As Imperialism*. Baltimore: Penguin Books, 1971.

Hirschman, Albert O., and Bird, Richard M. "Foreign Aid — A Critique and a Proposal." *Essays in International Finance*, no. 69, International Finance Section, Department of Economics, Princeton University. July 1968.

Huntington, Samuel. "Political Modernization: America vs. Europe." *World Politics* 18 (April 1966): 378-414.

Inter-American Development Bank Proceedings: Tenth Meeting of the Board of Governors. Guatemala (April 1969).

International Bank for Reconstruction and Development. *Annual Report*, 1974.

———. "Substitution of Labor for Equipment in Road Construction." Projects Department, Report no. TO-477 (May 1965).

———. *Transportation*. Sector Working Paper, January 1972.

———. *World Bank Staff Occasional Papers*. Baltimore: Johns Hopkins University Press.

Johnson, Harry G. "The 'Crisis of Aid' and The Pearson Report." A Lecture delivered at the University of Edinburgh on 6 iii 1970. Edinburgh: At the University Press, 1970.

Johnston, Bruce F., and Kilby, Peter. *Agriculture and Structural Transformation: Economic Strategies in Late Developing Countries*. London: Oxford University Press, 1975, forthcoming.

Kaplan, Jacob J. *The Challenge of Foreign Aid: Policies, Problems, and Possibilities*. New York: Praeger, 1967.

Lachman, Alexis E. *The Local Currency Proceeds of Foreign Aid*. Paris: OECD, 1968.

Lawrence, Paul R., and Lorsch, Jay W. *Developing Organizations: Diagnosis and Action*. Reading, Massachusetts: Addison-Wesley, 1969.

———. *Organization and Environment: Managing Differentiation and Integration*. Boston: Graduate School of Business Administration, Harvard University, 1967.

Leavitt, Harold. "Unhuman Organizations." *Harvard Business Review* 40 (July-August 1962): 90-98.

Levinson, Jerome, and de Onis, Juan. *The Alliance That Lost Its Way*. Chicago: Quadrangle Books, 1970.

McKibbin, Carroll. "Attrition of Foreign Service Officers: Then and Now." *Foreign Service Journal* 46 (May 1969).

McKinnon, Ronald I. *Money and Capital in Economic Development*. Washington, D.C.: The Brookings Institution, 1973.

———. "Foreign Exchange Constraints in Economic Development and Efficient Aid Allocation." *Economic Journal* 74 (June 1965): 388-409.

Maddison, Angus. *Foreign Skills and Technical Assistance in Economic Development*. Paris: Development Centre of the Organisation for Economic Co-operation and Development, 1965.

Mason, Edward S., and Asher, Robert E. *The World Bank Since Bretton Woods*. Washington, D.C.: The Brookings Institution, 1973.

Meerman, Jacob P. "Issues Concerning Capital Assistance to Less Developed Countries: Comment." *Economic Development and Cultural Change* 22 (January 1974): 338-44.

Mellor, John W., and Lele, Uma J. "Growth Linkages of the New Foodgrain Technologies." *Indian Journal of Agricultural Economics,* January-March 1973, pp. 35-55.

Mikesell, Raymond F. *The Economics of Foreign Aid.* Chicago: Aldine, 1968.

Montgomery, John D. *The Politics of Foreign Aid: American Experience in Southeast Asia.* New York: Praeger, 1962.

Morrow, William L. "Legislative Control of Administrative Discretion: The Case of Congress and Foreign Aid." *Journal of Politics* 30 (November 1968): 985-1011.

Mosher, Frederick C. "Some Observations about Foreign Service Reforms: 'Famous First Words.' " *Public Administration Review* 29 (November-December 1969): 600-613.

Nelson, Joan M. *Aid, Influence, and Foreign Policy.* New York: Macmillan Co., 1968.

Organisation for Economic Co-operation and Development. *Development Co-operation, 1973 Review.* Paris: OECD, 1973.

Organization of American States. *External Financing for Latin American Development.* Baltimore: Johns Hopkins Press, 1971.

Owens, Edgar, and Shaw, Robert. *Development Reconsidered: Bridging the Gap Between Government and People.* Lexington, Massachusetts: D. C. Heath and Company, 1972.

Pack, Howard. "Employment and Productivity in Kenyan Manufacturing." Institute for Development Studies, University of Nairobi. August 1972.

Papanek, Gustav F. "Aid, Foreign Private Investment, Savings, and Growth in Less Developed Countries." *Journal of Political Economy* 81 (January-February 1973): 120-30.

———. "The Effect of Aid and Other Resource Transfers on Savings and Growth in Less Developed Countries." *Economic Journal,* no. 327 (September 1972): 934-50.

Parkinson, C. Northcote. *Parkinson's Law and Other Studies in Administration.* Boston: Houghton Mifflin, 1957.

Patten, Richard; Dapice, Belinda; and Falcon, Walter. "An Experiment in Rural-Employment Creation: Indonesia's Kabupaten Development Program." n.d.

Peabody, Robert L., and Rourke, Francis E. "Public Bureaucracies." In *Handbook of Organizations,* edited by James G. March. Chicago: Rand McNally, 1965.

Perloff, Harvey S. *Alliance for Progress: A Social Invention in the Making.* Baltimore: Johns Hopkins Press, 1969.

Pickett, James; Forsyth, D. J. C.; and McBain, N. S. "The Choice of Technology, Economic Efficiency and Employment in Developing Countries." Xeroxed. Glasgow, February 1973.

Pincus, John. *Trade, Aid, and Development: The Rich and Poor Nations.* New York: McGraw-Hill, 1967.

Repetto, Robert. "Economic Aspects of Irrigation Project Design in East Pakistan." In *Development Policy II – The Pakistan Experience*, edited by Walter P. Falcon and Gustav F. Papenek. Cambridge: Harvard University Press, 1971.

Richardson, John M., Jr. *An Analysis of AID-University Relations, 1950-1966*. East Lansing: Michigan State University Press, 1969.

Rockefeller, Nelson A. *The Rockefeller Report on the Americas.* The Official Report of a United States Presidential Mission for the Western Hemisphere. Chicago: Quadrangle Books, 1969.

Rogers, William D. *The Twilight Struggle: The Alliance for Progress and the Politics of Development in Latin America.* New York: Random House, 1967.

Rosenstein-Rodan, P. N. "International Aid for Underdeveloped Countries." *The Review of Economics and Statistics* 43 (May 1961): 107-38.

Schelling, Thomas. "PPBS and Foreign Affairs." *Planning-Programming-Budgeting.* Inquiry of the Subcommittee on National Security and International Operations for the Committee on Government Operations of the U.S. Senate, pp. 111-20. Washington, D.C.: GPO, 1970.

Selznick, Philip. *TVA and the Grass Roots: A Study in the Sociology of Formal Organizations.* 1949 Reprint. New York: Harper Torchbooks, 1966.

Singer, H. W. "External Aid: For Plans or Projects?" *The Economic Journal* 75 (September 1965): 539-45.

Smelser, Neil J. *The Sociology of Economic Life.* Englewood Cliffs, New Jersey: Prentice-Hall, 1963.

Strout, Alan M., and Clark, Paul S. "Aid, Performance, Self-Help, and Need." A.I.D. Discussion Paper no. 20. July 1969.

Thomas, John W. "The Choice of Technology in Developing Countries: The Case of Irrigation Tubewells in Bangladesh." n.d.

———. "Rural Public Works and East Pakistan's Development." In *Development Policy II – The Pakistan Experience*, edited by Walter P. Falcon and Gustav F. Papanek. Cambridge: Harvard University Press, 1971.

Thompson, James D. *Organizations in Action: Social Science Bases of Administration Theory.* New York: McGraw-Hill, 1967.

Timmer, C. Peter. "Choice of Technique in Indonesia." Food Research Institute Discussion Paper no. 72-4. 1972.

Todd, John E. "Size of Firm and Efficiency in Colombian Manufacturing." Research Memorandum no. 41, Williams College Center for Development Economics. October 1971.

Toward A Modern Diplomacy: A Report to the American Foreign Service Association. Washington, D.C.: American Foreign Service Association, 1968.

Truman, David B. "The Domestic Politics of Foreign Aid." *Proceedings of the Academy of Political Science* 27 (January 1962): 62-72.

Tullock, Gordon. *The Politics of Bureaucracy.* Washington: Public Affairs Press, 1965.

United Nations Development Programme. *A Study of the United Nations Development System* (The Jackson Report). Geneva: United Nations, 1969.

United States Agency for International Development. Brazil Mission. Various Documents.

United States. Congress. House of Representatives. Committee on Appropriations. *Foreign Assistance and Related Agencies, Appropriations for 1971*, part 2. Hearings Before the Subcommittee on Foreign Operations and Related Agencies. 91st Cong., 2d sess., 18 March 1970.

———. *Foreign Assistance and Related Agencies, Appropriations for 1973*, part 2. Hearings Before the Subcommittee on Foreign Operations and Related Agencies. 92d Cong., 2d sess., 25 April 1972.

———. *Foreign Assistance and Related Agencies, Appropriations for 1974*, part 2. Hearings Before the Subcommittee on Foreign Operations and Related Agencies. 93d Cong., 1st sess., 10 June 1973.

———. *Foreign Assistance and Related Agencies, Appropriations for 1975*, part 2. Hearings Before the Subcommittee on Foreign Operations and Related Agencies. 93d Cong., 2d sess., 3 June 1974.

———. *Foreign Assistance and Related Programs, Appropriations for 1975*. Report of the House Subcommittee on Foreign Operations and Related Agencies. 94th Cong., 1st sess., H. Rep. 94-53.

United States. Congress. House of Representatives. Committee on Foreign Affairs. *Foreign Assistance Act of 1969*, parts 5 and 6. Hearings Before the Committee on Foreign Affairs. 91st Cong., 1st sess., 14 July and 22 July 1969.

———. *Foreign Assistance for the 'Seventies*. Message from the President of the United States Proposing a Transformation of Foreign Assistance Programs. 91st Cong., 2d sess., H. Doc. 91-385. 15 September 1970.

———. *New Directions for the 1970's: Toward A Strategy of Inter-American Development*. Hearings Before the Subcommittee on Inter-American Affairs. 91st Cong., 1st sess., 25 February 1969.

United States. Congress. Joint Economic Committee. *A Review of Balance of Payments Policies*. Hearings Before the Subcommittee on International Exchange and Payments. 91st Cong., 1st sess., 13 January 1969.

United States. Congress. Senate. Committee on Appropriations. *Personnel Administration and Operations of Agency for International Development*. Report of Senator Gale W. McGee to the Committee on Appropriations. 88th Cong., 1st sess., S. Doc. 57. 29 November 1963.

———. *Personnel Administration and Operations of Agency for International Development*. Special Hearings Before the Committee on Appropriations. 88th Cong., 1st sess., 8 May 1963.

United States. Congress. Senate. Committee on Foreign Relations. *Foreign Economic Assistance, 1973*. Hearings Before the Committee on Foreign Relations. 93d Cong., 1st sess., 26 June 1973.

United States. Department of State. *Diplomacy for the 70's: A Program of Management Reform for the Department of State*. Department of State Publication 8551, Department and Foreign Service Series 143. Washington, D.C.: GPO, 1970.

United States. President. Task Force on Foreign Economic Assistance. *An Act* for *International Development: A Program for the Decade of Development, Fiscal Year 1962.* Summary Presentation, General Foreign Policy Series no. 169. Washington, D.C.: U.S. Department of State, 1961.

United States. President. Task Force on International Development. *U.S. Foreign Assistance in the 1970's: A New Approach* (The Peterson Report). Report to the President from the Task Force on International Development. Washington, D.C.: GPO, 1970.

Wall, David. *The Charity of Nations: The Political Economy of Foreign Aid.* New York: Basic Books, 1973.

Wells, Louis T., Jr. "Economic Man and Engineering Man: Choice of Technology in a Low Wage Country." Economic Development Report no. 266, Harvard University Center for International Affairs. November 1972.

White, John. *Regional Development Banks: The Asian, African and Inter-American Banks.* New York: Praeger, 1972.

Wilson, James Q. "Innovation in Organization: Notes Toward A Theory." In *Approaches to Organizational Design,* edited by James D. Thompson. Pittsburgh: University of Pittsburgh Press, 1966.

Wood, Robert E. "When Government Works." *The Public Interest* 18 (Winter 1970).

INDEX

ABDIB, 59

Abundance of development assistance: avoidance of, 96-97; effect of, on import cost financing, 55, 79; effect of, on resource allocation, 55, 56; effect of, on size of aid projects, 56; effect of on type of loan, 57; and recipient-country financial market, 98; scarcity versus, 54

"Additionality" requirements, 45, 47

Agricultural development, 106-8

AID: accountability of, 42; bureaucracy in, 3-4; comparison of, with multilateral agencies, 4; decentralization in, 12, 13, 25, 26, 36; decline of, 6; and federal agencies, 44-45, 48; goals in, 49-50; Latin American program of, 5; loans to Brazil by, 58-59, 65, 68-69; mission rotation in, 14, 21; money-moving behavior in, 88-90; organizational environment of, 8, 23, 36-37; relations of, with Congress, 12-13, 16; restrictions on, 40-42; Washington-mission conflicts in, 26, 30; writing in, 50-53. See also AID personnel; Constraints on AID activities; Criticism of AID

AID personnel: characteristics of, 12-13, 17; isolation of, overseas, 27-31, 33-34; medical care of, 31; morale of, 29; privileges and allowances of, 31-36; promotion policy for, 17; social cohesiveness of, 28-30; temporary status of, 14, 15, 16-17, 18-19, 20

Alliance for Progress, 19, 27

American Foreign Service Association, 18

Army Post Office (APO), 31, 32

Balance of payments: additionality procedures and, 45; effect of AID on, 45, 49; foreign aid and, 44, 47, 48

Bilateral aid: by AID, 3, 4; political and business interference with, 2. See also AID

Blau, Peter M., 29

Brazil, 5; CANAMBRA power studies for, 63-64; equipment manufacturing in, 72; highway maintenance equipment loan to, 68-69; proposed AID equipment loan to, 47. See also Passo Real hydroelectric power plant

Budget Bureau, 44

CANAMBRA, 63-64

Capital: allocation of, 98; deemphasis of, 100; extravagant use of, 99

Capital-intensive projects: bias toward, 56, 100-101, 108; import financing and, 75, 105; status of technology and, 77. See also Technology, labor using

Commerce Department, 44, 45, 46, 48

Congress, U.S.: AID funding by, 12-13, 16; inquiries into AID activities by, 49, 50, 51

Constraints on AID activities: by checks on expenditures, 40-42; by Federal agencies, 24-25, 38, 44-47, 48; by financing policies, 55-56; legal versus institutional, 49-50; legislative, 43-44; by Washington staff, 23-24

Cost-benefit analysis, 93, 97

Criticism of AID: by beneficiaries, 43; for collusion with U.S. business interests, 48; displacement of goals as result of, 49-50; effect of, on agency activities, 40; for equipment loan to Brazil, 47;

Library of Congress Cataloging in Publication Data

Tendler, Judith.
  Inside foreign aid.

  Bibliography: p. 129
  Includes index.
  1. Economic assistance, American. I. Title.
HC60.T47   338.91'172'4073   75-11353
ISBN 0-8018-1731-5
ISBN 0-8018-2016-2 (paperback)